ART OF THE UPSET

ART OF THE UPSET

Bruce Reynolds

Don,
To a great Coach,
great person and
to a good Friend.
Hope you enjoy the
book.

Bruce Reynolds

ADVOCATE HOUSE   *SARASOTA FLORIDA*

For information regarding permissions, write to:
A Cappela Publishing
P. O. Box 3691
Sarasota FL 34230-3691

LIBRARY OF CONGRESS CATALOGING-IN-PUBLICATION DATA
Reynolds, Bruce
Art of the Upset / Bruce Reynolds
p. cm.
ISBN 978- 0-9818933-6-5
1. Sports and Recreation   2. Games   3. Self-help

First Edition

Printed in Canada

ACKNOWLEDGMENTS

I would like to thank the following people for their contributions to the writing of this book. First, I owe a sincere debt of gratitude to my family for their support and for providing me with many of the principles that I have outlined in the *Art of The Upset*. My football mentor, colleague and friend Bill L. Cole, helped mold my coaching philosophy and coaching career. My undying gratitude also goes to my outstanding assistant coaches who unselfishly brought their skill, enthusiasm and loyalty to our program.

The players that I had the privilege to coach gave more to me than I could have ever given to them. They have given me memories that will last a lifetime. Thanks to all of the parents, Boosters, and fans of the Colonial School District's William Penn High School, and to its administration and board of education.

On the technical side, thanks go to Nancy Freebery for her book cover design and website work. A final and special thank-you goes to Pat Taylor, whose editorial skills, suggestions, and eye for detail were critical in putting this book in final form.

FOREWORD

I would like to state clearly from the start that this book is a result of a lifetime of interaction with thousands of people. I have benefited from books, lectures, conferences, sermons, and a host of personal experiences and observations. When I speak of success, I have tried to be careful; it is all too easy to fall into the "I" syndrome, but it is clear to me that any success that I have ever had has not been done alone. I have benefited from nurturing and supportive parents, family, friends, teachers, colleagues, coaches, and players. *Art of the Upset* is a compilation of these influences. Where I have written a reference to myself and used the "I" word, please mentally substitute the word "we."

I also want to make clear for the record that I have had the good fortune to lose big games as well as win them. I say "good fortune" because it was in the losses that I gained the most knowledge on how to win. This book, however, is not just about how to win the big games. It is more about how to develop a program and a philosophy that make the upsets possible. The mark of a successful program is consistency, but consistency cannot be maintained if you can't win the games you're supposed to win, and win some of those program-defining games that all coaches dream of pulling off – the upset.

I was a head football coach for 27 years; therefore, I have derived most of my illustrations from my chosen sport. However, the philosophy of the book applies to all sports and, I believe, to any chosen profession. I have also applied the methods and philosophy described in this book to my 31-year career as a social studies teacher; my 4-year career as the Coordinator of Community Relations for the Colonial School District; my 17 years as an Assistant Athletic Director; my 18-year career as a State of Delaware Representative and chairman of the House Education Committee, and my 35-plus-year career as a banquet emcee and motivational speaker. The lessons learned in all of these endeavors are reflected in this book. My goal is to share with you the core philosophy that will enable you to pull off the big upset and to offer something in this book that will be of help to you and your career. If you are a coach, try some of the things that my staff and I have learned through trial and error. Who knows? One idea learned here just might be the catalyst for that long-desired and dreamed-of upset of your archrival.

THE UPSET

The quarterback scrambles from the fierce rush, time running out. He gathers himself and heaves a desperation pass toward the streaking end. The defenders close in and simultaneously leap high in the air with the receiver. Hands stretch out and grab for the ball. The gun sounds to end the game as the players fall to the ground. Who caught the ball? Did we win . . . ?

As painful as it is sometimes, nothing compares to the emotional highs and lows of sports. Life at times meanders along with very little that truly excites us, but there are those times in sports when our emotions are jolted into high gear. Nothing moves the player, coach or fan more than the upset. It is that indescribable thrill that engulfs you when no one thinks you can do something and you do it. It becomes that one time when sacrifice, hard work, and belief in self and team collide into an explosion of high emotion. It is a phenomenon when time itself seems to momentarily stand still and one feels most alive. For the coach, player, or die-hard fan, it is a time when you put your passion, your talent, your whole being on the line for all to witness. When that long pass with seconds to go is sailing through the air and your heart is in your throat, nothing else exists.

It's a moment of truth that will end in great exultation or bitter disappointment. Some can't stand living on the edge like that. But there is something in all of us that lives for that one-in-a-million time when the ball is caught with no time on the clock and your team wins! How I loved and lived for those moments! But what I enjoyed even more was the process that made that upset possible.

How does a coach instill in his players that "come from behind" approach to competition? You might think that calling that last-minute play was a stroke of genius on the part of the coach. Maybe it was! But really, the process of winning that game had begun months before, even seasons before the game was played. The victory was the result of a coaching mind-set I like to call the "art of the upset."

WHERE UPSETS BEGIN

Upsets truly begin in the mind. Your eyes and ears will deceive you. When you rationally look at a bigger, stronger opponent, you don't think that you could beat them. If you listen to the writers, the fans, and their take on your chances, you certainly don't think that you could possibly win. That's why the image of the upset must begin in your mind. Your mind can defy the rational. It can block the visual and auditory reality. Your mind's eye can be programmed to see a victory that others cannot see.

There is a blueprint that, if followed, can give you the edge you need to win. If David had let his eyes rule the day, there would be no story of a slain Goliath. He was too big, too strong, and too well-armored. But David had faith. In his mind's eye he could win. As a matter of fact, his confidence was so strong he did not believe that he could lose! Players and coaches have to take a leap of faith in order to win when the opposition is formidable. To re-word a Napoleon Hill axiom: You have to think it and believe it before you can achieve it.

James Allen, in his book *As a Man Thinketh,* confirms my own belief in this principle. He says, "Every thought-seed sown or allowed to fall into the mind, and to take root there, produces its own, blossoming sooner or later into act, and bearing its own fruitage of opportunity and circumstance. Good thoughts bear good fruit, bad thoughts bad fruit." That is probably a take-off on a quote from Shakespeare's *Hamlet*: "There is nothing either good or bad, but thinking makes it so." So be careful of what thoughts you put in your head and plant in the minds of your players!

BE CAREFUL

Be careful of your thoughts
For thoughts become your word.
Be careful of your words
For your words become your actions.
Be careful of your actions
For your actions become your habits.
Be careful of your habits
For your habits become your character.
Be careful of your character
For your character becomes your destiny.
(Author Unknown)

James Allen also contends, "Man is buffeted by circumstance as long as he believes himself to be the creature of outside conditions." His point is that circumstances come out of thought. If you can program yourself to believe in your self, your team, and your goal, you can and will create the climate for success. You will create the intended result by sheer will power. You can therefore change negative circumstances into positive ones. It is all centered in your thoughts. For me, as location is to real estate, thought is to victory. For James Allen, the idea that circumstances grow out of thought has its proof with anyone who has tried this approach. He states that the person "will have noticed that the alteration in his circumstances has been in exact ratio with his altered mental condition."

Here is a little exercise that demonstrates how your change of mental focus can change what you see. Hold out your hand and look at it closely. Your eyes see the hand clearly and everything else in the distance is blurry and unclear. Now, change your focus to a distant object. That object automatically comes into focus and your hand becomes blurred and out of focus. You can, at will, go back and forth between the two. The analogy is simple. You determine at will what you see and therefore what you think. It's all about what you choose to focus on. If you focus on the negative reality of your circumstances, you won't see the positive. You won't see the upset. To pull off the upset, you have to change the focus and see only the positive.

Sometimes you have to create the positives in your imagination. The bottom line is that to avoid seeing only the external reality of your situation, you have to create your own internal reality. Ralph S. Marston, Jr. in *The Daily Motivator to Go*, relates, "The mind thinks about 60,000 thoughts a day." So just by "sheer volume" you can see that your thoughts will have a huge impact on your life. He goes on to say, "Success is an inside job." You can think positive thoughts, or you can think negative and limiting ones. You actually have a choice. Why do you think it is so hard to get a team who is used to losing to change its ways? They are mired in a negative-thinking mindset. Marston gives a great illustration to show this point. He talks about how juvenile elephants are trained. Baby elephants are tethered to a four-foot wooden stake driven into the ground. They repeatedly try to pull away from the stake, but to no avail. After hundreds of attempts they simply stop trying. This carries over into their adult life as well. How can you explain that 6 to 8-ton elephants cannot pull out 4-foot long wooden stakes? The explanation is simple: they stopped trying. In their mind they "know" that they cannot get free, so they don't even try. That's why a comparatively puny trainer can control a 12,000 – pound (or more) powerhouse. His lesson for us is, "When you believe in what you're doing, and believe that you can do it, you'll find a way to make it happen."

You need to get your team to see that, in Marston's words, "The reality of the outside world is only a mirror. A mirror that confirms and gives evidence to the vision that you have on the inside." Your job is to get your team to create their own internal vision – their own positive internal reality. Remember, external facts (i.e., the other team is bigger, faster, stronger, better, undefeated, etc.) may be the external reality. But they must mentally ignore that and concentrate on their own created, positive-outcome vision. Their "reality" must tell them that if they work hard, never quit, execute with precision, and play inspired team ball, they will win the game. The poet Maya Angelou wrote, "If one is lucky, a solitary fantasy can totally transform one million realities." We followed up that thought with the adage, "The harder we work the luckier we get!" Remember, upsets do happen and that is where they begin – right in your own mind!

FOCUS

Once you have planted in your players' minds thought seeds to victory (the vision), you must now teach them how to put those thoughts into action. Thought without action is like keeping your car in neutral – you just won't get anywhere. Having the vision will not be enough. Your players will have to sustain their vision (goals) throughout the entire game or better yet, the entire season. You should teach them that there are many ways to do this; it all starts, however, with focus.

I previously mentioned focus and what you choose to focus on as keys to pulling off the upset. However, the intensity of the focus and the ability to stay focused are also paramount. Jeffrey Smith, in his book *Focus on Your Dream*, states, "If there is one thing I've learned over the years, it's that the fine line between those who win and those who don't is what they focus on. Winners stay focused on what they want and continually take action to move themselves closer to their dream. Everyone else doesn't." The focus on the opponent cannot be like shining a flashlight on an object. The flashlight approach is too broad. The light is diffused. But the laser is penetrating and precise. It allows for a tunnel-vision approach to fulfilling your goals. So trade in your flashlight for a laser. Only an intense focus on beating a particular opponent will do the job.

You must first get your team's attention and then demand that they embrace the idea that you can win the "big one." Henry Ford once said, "If you believe you can do a thing, or you believe you cannot, you're probably right." The roots of this philosophy are biblical: "All things are possible to him that believeth" (Mark 9.23). Give them the vision; then and only then do you start doing the things that will convince them that they can win.

Without a clear goal or vision, not much will be accomplished. Jeffrey Smith, in *Focus on Your Dream*, uses the acronym "ITIFAR" to help remember how this process works. You are "Inspired" to create "Thoughts" which form "Images" which lead to "Feelings" that determine your "Actions" which give you your "Results." We always called this "buying in" to the program. Unless your team "buys in," there is slim chance of consistent success and pulling off the big game upsets.

Ralph S. Marston, Jr. in his book *The Daily Motivator to Go*, contends that success will only be found through consistent and persistent effort. But first you have to develop in yourself and your players the "now" concept. Marston states that your success will not be ". . . found in the fondly remembered past. It is also not in the hoped for future. It is here and now." He adds, "Anything that may have previously held you back is now behind you. Today is your golden opportunity to fashion your life . . . (and your team) into what you want it to be." It is the timeless philosophy that you cannot always control the situation or the circumstances you find yourself in, but you can control how you look at those circumstances.

You can control your perception, and therefore, the direction of your efforts to deal with your circumstance. This is critical to the team that does not have a winning heritage. It is also critical to a particular team that is not getting the hoped for success in any given season. A two- or three-game losing streak can become a four- or five-game losing streak easily. You must find the way to reach your team and get them to believe in their ability to win. Start today! The one little thing that you do extra today may be the very thing that will bring you success. Make your players believe that the one extra sprint at the end of practice may be the difference in prevailing in the fourth quarter. They must "buy in" that the one extra repetition of a block will be the one that springs the back for the winning touchdown.

I have previously mentioned Napoleon Hill's famous saying, "Whatever the mind can conceive and believe, the mind can achieve." That saying occupies a prominent place in our weight room. Dr. Norman Vincent Peale further popularized this concept in *The Power of Positive Thinking*. Peale called it "imaging." He contends that imaging consists of " . . . vividly picturing, in your conscious mind, a desired goal or objective, and holding that image until it sinks into your unconscious mind, where it releases great untapped energies. . . . When the imaging concept is applied steadily and systematically, it . . . greatly enhances the chances for success in any kind of endeavor."

The modern athlete who best exemplifies the ability to visualize and intensely focus is Tiger Woods. No one does it better! Just listen to his own words after winning the 2008 Arnold Palmer Invitational Tournament by sinking a 25-foot putt on the final hole to win by one stroke. Tiger recalled, "I was so into the moment of the putt going in and winning the golf tournament. I kept telling myself, I've done this before. . . . I've done it before and I can do it again." Tiger is so focused that later in the year he was able to gut out and endure five grueling days of golf to win the U.S. Open in a play-off with Rocco Mediate. I say gut out and endure because Tiger played the entire tournament on a damaged knee and fractured leg!

Whether you call it "the power of positive thinking," "guided imaging," or "creative visualization" won't matter. What will matter is that you share this philosophy with your team and apply its principles. You will have nothing to lose and everything to gain. Try it; it works!

KEEP YOUR FOCUS AND OVERCOME OBSTACLES WITH "SURGE"

Turn negative signs into positive outcomes. You must instill within your players the idea that they must overcome all negatives with increased determination and focus. We called that "surge." We practiced "surge" all of the time. Create negative situations for your players. Remind them that they must "surge" to overcome them. They must step it up a notch to wipe out the negative. They must embrace the belief that no obstacle will deter them from their goal. We tried to capture the idea that obstacles were just necessary components to our quest for success. They provided opportunities for our team to expand and grow. Our approach to them was simple — hard work. The great industrialist, Henry Kaiser, once summed up this philosophy when he said, "Obstacles are only opportunities in work clothes."

The road to success is always strewn with obstacles. So don't fear them; embrace them. The process of working through and solving them will become the milestones on your journey to the top. Dream big. Why not? Never let the obstacles you see before you limit your goals. You think you have obstacles? What about Wilbur and Orville

Wright? They even had to overcome one of the strongest forces in nature – gravity! And, don't let anyone tell you or your team that they can't do it. A man by the name of Brutus Hamilton wrote about what he called the ultimate levels that man could reach physically. His letters focused on what man would never be able to accomplish– levels beyond which men could not go. Hamilton was a famous Olympic athlete and later coach of the 1952 U.S. Olympic track team. In his writings at that time he said that the "dream mile" was "beyond human endurance," and, the fastest possible time in which a man could run a mile was 4:01.66 minutes. At about the same time, Jake Weber, a famous track coach at Fordham, came to the same conclusion. He said, "There will never be a four minute mile. A man's heart will not stand it, and that's all there is to it."

It is interesting to note that what was thought to be the limits to the fastest times run, the greatest heights jumped, and the fastest times swum, are all being broken now by high school (and in some cases even junior high) athletes. Of course, I know you have to set reasonable goals, but allow yourself and your team to "dream big" without fear of the obstacles blocking the path. Remember, without obstacles to overcome, there is no joy in accomplishment. The more numerous and severe the obstacles the more pride in accomplishment there will be. What joy is there in doing something that requires no sacrifice or effort? Booker T. Washington once said, "You measure the size of the accomplishment by the obstacles you had to overcome to reach your goals." There has never been an upset that was not accompanied by the overcoming of many problems and frustrations. As Frank A. Clark put it so aptly, "If you can find a path with no obstacles, it probably doesn't lead anywhere."

Knowing that we would always be faced with obstacles allowed us the opportunity to prepare for them and actually embrace them.

Our team didn't fear them because we knew that we would overcome them with our "surge" mentality. Whenever something bad happened to our team during a game, we would yell "Surge!" to flip a switch in our thinking and "amp up" our aggressive play. The word simply meant to us to forget what just happened, concentrate only on the next play, and pick up the intensity (increase the passion). The word had to be programmed into our subconscious so that we didn't have to think about it – only react.

The idea for "surge" came to us after a painful loss. We were playing in the state semi-final championship game and holding a truly strong and well-coached team to a 6 – 6 tie with six minutes left in the game. We had kept an All-State running back (Mike Meade, who later played professional football) under control. What happened next, however, swung the momentum and the game to our opponent. We had held them to short yardage on first and second down. On third down they threw a deep pass that sailed high over their receiver and our defender. There was no contact visible, and the film supports this clearly. However, a late flag was thrown against us for pass interference, giving our opponents an automatic first down. I was so incensed I couldn't see straight. My team took their cue from me and was visibly upset. My focus and theirs was completely on the injustice of the call. When the team lined up to run the next play, we were all still brooding about the bad call.

You can probably guess what happened next. Their great running back broke off a long run for a touchdown. That touchdown shortly resulted in another touchdown, and we lost the game. Even after they scored on that long run, we were still upset over the bad call. Our opponent was good and might have eventually won the game anyway, but I am convinced that my, and therefore my team's misdirected focus led to a downward spiral from which we did not recover. For me the loss was a direct result of our reaction to the negative call.

That experience birthed our "Surge" philosophy. From that point on we actually set up negative practice situations that forced our team to "surge." For example, have your first team defense stop your practice offense for four downs and go off the field proud of their accomplishment. Immediately send in your first team offense and instruct them to fumble the ball on the first play and not recover it. Your first team defense has to come right back onto the field and start all over again. When I was in college, I saw first hand what could happen in this circumstance in a tight game. The defensive players were upset with the offense, and words were exchanged. Great for team morale isn't it? "One for all and all for one" goes right out the door. Focus is lost, and usually the game with it. I vowed then that if I ever coached, that would not be the case. The "surge" philosophy does not allow any negative thoughts following that type of incident. The focus is immediately on "upping" your focus and your energy level for the next play.

We also had our team run plays and score and have our referee-coach call the touchdown back for holding or some other infraction (whether it had occurred or not). The team was not allowed to think about the bad call. The rest of the team and the coaches immediately started yelling at the top of our lungs, "Surge!" Practice running plays after a fumble, bad call, interception, offsides, a sack, delay of game, and any and all negative plays that you can think up. When you do this repeatedly over the course of the season, it will instill in your team the ability to recover from adversity and to do it immediately with renewed enthusiasm. They will learn the secret of how to take a negative situation and turn it into a positive force. It is a key ingredient in the "art of the upset."

The ability to find a positive side to a negative experience was illuminated for me by my father, Dr. Brooks E. Reynolds – after his death in 2004. Dad had enjoyed a long career as a Methodist minister, and shortly after his death I lost an election for the Delaware State House of Representatives (after 18 years of service) by only 22 votes. Three months later, I received a letter from Dad. (My brother Brooks had found it in some of Dad's papers.) It was unnerving. It was as if my father knew I had lost the election. My lingering disappointment was mollified by his selection of the passage from Corinthians 2, 5.17. The essence of the passage tells us, "The old has gone, the new has come." Game translation: you can't dwell on what just happened (good or bad) in the game. You must concentrate and focus on the next play and then the next. Studies have shown that the key to good leadership is in the recovery time – the time it takes for a leader to assess a negative situation and move on into a positive response. I viscerally know this to be true. If "surge" had been a part of our mindset in that semi-final loss, who knows what the outcome would have been? I know for certain that at least we would have had a chance to win.

Josh Waitzkin, in his book *The Art of Learning*, talks about this same subject in the context of competitive chess. Josh's story is the basis for the true-life version of the book (and later, film) *Searching for Bobby Fischer*. Josh's father, Freddy Waitzkin, wrote the book chronicling his son's rise to early competitive chess super stardom. Josh won his first national chess championship at the age of nine. He later went on to win world chess championships and also world championships in Tai Chi martial arts – a champion in two distinctly different endeavors. Yet his approach was the same for both when it came to overcoming adverse circumstances and making them work for you.

Waitzkin talks of his understanding of the difference between winning and losing. He says, "The distance between the two is minute, and, moreover, there are ways to steal wins from the maw of defeat." One of his main themes is " . . . the importance of regaining presence and clarity of mind after making a serious error." He continues, "This is a hard lesson for all competitors and performers. The first mistake rarely proves disastrous, but the downward spiral of the second, third, and fourth error creates a devastating chain reaction." He emphasizes the phenomenon of "momentum" in every aspect of competition. Momentum is a key component of every football game and every other form of competition. Waitzkin observes that some competitors " . . . fall to pieces . . . " when they make their first mistake. They become so consumed by the error that they are not mentally free to tackle the next move or play. Shackled by this mindset they make another and then another error. The "downward spiral" (negative momentum) then claims another victim.

Waitzkin contends that the key is to have your players ride " . . . the psychological wave when it is behind you, and snapping back into a fresh presence when your clarity of mind begins to be swept away." For me that's "surge." Josh Waitzkin taught his students to be "present at critical moments of competition." He gave them strategies to do this. He would stop and go out and run wind sprints and then go back to the chessboard. He taught his students to stop and take three deep breaths or splash cold water on their face – anything to stop, regroup their thoughts and start fresh with a renewed focus. Waitzkin had witnessed an accident in New York City traffic. A woman stepped into the street while looking to her right. A bicycle rider coming from her left swerved sharply and grazed her. She received a small bump, nothing serious. The woman was so incensed at the rider that she turned toward him and began to curse him. Had she just gathered herself and stepped back onto the pavement the one error would not have been a devastating one. Instead she lost it; while cursing the rider, she did not see the taxicab coming around the curve. The taxi struck her from behind and sent her a good ten feet into the air. She flew into a lamppost and was knocked out and bleeding. Injured but still alive, she was taken to a nearby hospital.

Josh was shaken by this tragic event. It left an indelible impression on him that helped formulate his philosophy of how to stay focused when bad things happen. In a football game, we would call a time-out and try to refocus. However, you only get a limited number of time-outs in a game. I hated to waste them on this, but if I had to, I did. Our approach was to use "Surge!" as our re-focus word. That one small word meant volumes to us. It meant forget about what just happened. Re-focus. Ratchet your level of enthusiasm and hustle and make something good happen right now – this very next play.

This is not easy to do. It is hard to overcome negative emotions sometimes. I shared what happened to me in the game we lost because I did not deal with negativity in a positive manner. But how about you? How do you deal with negative situations or defeat? Have you ever had the proverbial wind knocked out of your gut by a bad play or a lost game? It feels the same as if a boxer had just laid his best body shot to your mid-section.

This happens to me all the time. It happens when I'm watching a game on TV as well. The discomfort is so overwhelming that I have to leave the room or change the channel. Has anyone ever learned how to truly harness those sinking multiple emotions: anger, frustration and guilt? You feel anger and frustration at the team, the coaches, the referees, the opponent, and a sense of guilt that you let a game of sport affect you on such a negative level. For a coach, however, the degree of those feelings and the recovery time is what will set apart the good coach from the merely adequate one. The good coach recovers quickly–in thought, word, and deed.

Your players have the same emotions. So how do you handle it? The best way is to accept the words of Wendell Phillips, who said, "What is defeat–nothing but education, nothing but the first step to something better." I took that to heart and learned from my mistakes. That's why we made "surge" a part of our mental and physical reaction to the ups and downs of a game. I strongly suggest that you try this approach with your team. It truly paid dividends for us.

LEARN TO LOSE
IN ORDER TO WIN

Don't make winning your primary goal. Your ultimate goal for your team should be to have them play their best. When you play only to win you create what author Josh Waitzkin calls " . . . the brittle dependence on perfection." If that is your goal, then when an error occurs, Waitzkin concludes, "[It] triggers fear, detachment, uncertainty, or confusion that muddies the decision-making process." In football I have seen teams lose because they became hesitant. They are so fearful of making a mistake that they focus more on "not losing" than on playing to their maximum capability. This creates situations where they do not respond to game conditions with spontaneity.

Your players must be trained to react to situations, however, and they need to react reflexively. For example, Coach Billy Cole, my mentor, always taught our defensive backs to read certain keys. We took a three-step drop on the snap while reading the keys. When the key was "run," they were to plant their foot, move up immediately, and force or contain the running game. When the key was "pass," they would drop to their specific zones and read the quarterback. This approach is effective because when a player is focused on not making a mistake, he becomes indecisive. Instead of reacting to his read, he thinks about the consequences of a possible mistake. He freezes in the moment. He doesn't come up quickly enough to stop the run, and when a receiver streaks deep, he is usually flat-footed and left behind. The results either way are never good. Bill was a master of teaching how to overcome this. I learned a lot from his mindset and approach to teaching this aspect of the game.

You have to be fearless and decisive as a competitor. You cannot play to "not lose." It just doesn't work. It is really counter-intuitive. It doesn't sound right to say that you have to lose in order to win; but you do have to *be willing* to lose in order to win. Great athletes and great teams must be willing to lose in order to win. This paradox is at the heart of winning competition.

For example, Michael Jordan was willing to "put himself on the line" in order to be great. Jordan made more last minute heroic buzzer-beater shots to win games than any other NBA player in history. Yet it is a lesser-known fact that he missed more game-ending shots than any other player. As Josh Waitzkin observes in *The Art of Learning,* "What made him the greatest was not perfection, but a willingness to put himself on the line as a way of life." He did not think of the possible negative consequences of those last-second shots. He knew what it would take to win and he instinctively did it. He didn't play to "not lose." He trusted in his coaching, his hours of practice, his skill and his ultimate faith in himself. Jordan said, "I have missed more than 9,000 shots in my career. I have lost almost 300 games. On 26 occasions I have been entrusted to take the game-winning shot . . . and I missed. I have failed over and over and over again in my life. And that's precisely why I succeed." Sales trainer Tom Hopkins, author of twelve books, including *How to Master the Art of*

Selling, would concur with Michael Jordan. Hopkins once said, "I am not judged by the number of times I fail, but by the number of times I succeed. And the number of times I succeed is in direct proportion to the number of times I can fail and keep trying."

We all make mistakes, but we always preached to our teams that if you make a mistake, make it aggressively – just like Mike! Michael Jordan was not afraid to fail. He was also not afraid of the critics. He was always a winner even when he lost, and that is our definition of winning. Winning for us was always about making the maximum effort and then letting the chips fall where they will.

You will not always win the big game. By its very definition the word "upset" denotes a special one-of-a-kind and sometimes once-in-a-lifetime event. Knowing this, the emphasis must be on the process and the effort. Set your goal high, and fiercely pursue it. Be fearless, and never concern yourself with what others may perceive as failure. It is never failure when you give your all.

As a former history teacher, I have always admired the courage of President Teddy Roosevelt. His "It's not the critic who counts" speech has always been an inspiration to me personally. My careers as a football coach, teacher and state representative often exposed me to severe criticism – some justified, some not. The consolation I always took when things did not work out the way I would have liked can be summed up in Teddy Roosevelt's answer to his critics, delivered in a speech entitled "Citizenship in a Republic." The full text of the speech is included in Roosevelt's book *History as Literature:*

> It is not the critic who counts, not the man who points out how the strong man stumbled, or where the doer of deeds could have done better. The credit belongs to the man who is actually in the arena; whose face is marred by

the dust and sweat and blood; who strives valiantly; who errs and comes short again and again; who knows the great enthusiasms, the great devotions, and spends himself in a worthy course; who at the best, knows in the end of the triumph of high achievement, and who, at worst, if he fails, at least fails while daring greatly; so that his place shall never be with those cold and timid souls who know neither victory nor defeat.

As long as I knew that I personally, along with our staff and players, gave it our all-out maximum effort, then I was satisfied. I would be disappointed for sure, but not devastated or defeated in spirit. Some of my most satisfying moments in coaching came from games we lost. I can still recall several losing games to powerhouse teams like Newark and Salesianum with great pride, the kind of pride that comes only from great effort! Remember the Alamo? Enough said!

PICKED TO WIN

I f you are ever picked to win the big game, you have extra work to do. Preparing your team to avoid being upset is often harder than getting them up to pull off the upset. Players sometime get complacent. They don't always feel the urgency necessary to prepare for the game that they are "supposed" to win easily. The fear of losing is a powerful motivator. If you lessen that fear psychologically, you may lessen the intensity needed to win the game.

As the coach, you have to point out the obvious: For every great upset there was a great team that was beaten. There was in each situation a Goliath who went down. You must make them aware of this fact of competitive life. The expected outcome does not always occur. Remember, the early bird gets the worm; however, conversely the early worm gets eaten by the bird. Another one of my favorites is, "Rome wasn't built in a day, but it was burned down in one." Every action has a reaction. For every upset there is a beaten team that should not have lost. The difference is easy to see in hindsight: the mindset of the winner v. the mindset of the loser. One believes and works to achieve the goal; the other quite possibly goes through the motions relying on past achievement and raw talent to get them through.

Thank goodness sports contests do not always go to the stronger man or team! That's why we play the game. How much fun would it be if it were always a given who would win? I sat down to watch the 2002 Super Bowl and expected to see the Rams win. The New England Patriots thought otherwise. I actually knew in my heart that something was different about that game right from the beginning. When the Patriots came out for the pre-game introduction they were not individually introduced. The Patriots were by choice introduced as a team. They were united in their goal to win the Super Bowl. They were right! No one individual was responsible for that upset. It was a total team effort from start to finish. Because of that mindset for the upset, the 2002 game will go down as one of the most interesting and entertaining in Super Bowl history.

EFFORT DEFINES WINNING
AND LOSING

You must have no fear of failure. The only way to win the upset is to give everything with no reservation. You cannot think about losing. It must be blocked from your consciousness. Only through this type of focus can you possibly win. To paraphrase Henry Ford again: "If you think you can win, or if you think you can't win, you'll probably be right." As Lonny Starr once said, "No matter what happens, there's always somebody who knew it would." What's the worst-case scenario for giving your all? You might lose! If you give everything and still lose the game, in my mind you are a winner. Your effort brands you and your team.

No one wants to lose, but life teaches us that even the best teams over the years will eventually lose. How you respond to the loss is the key. In 1964, Clifton Cushman, the University of Kansas track star, was preparing himself for Olympic glory. During the U.S. Olympic trials Cushman hit the last hurdle – a crushing blow. To put it in his own words, he fell " . . . in an inglorious heap of skinned elbows, bruised hips, torn knees and injured pride." His spirit could have been broken, but it wasn't. He was disappointed for sure, but

26

not broken. Many family, friends, and fellow competitors called and wrote to Clifton. He responded with the true spirit of the competitor. He replied to all with "An Open Letter to Young People." In the letter he wrote:

> In a split second, the years of training, pain, sweat, blisters and agony of running were . . . wiped out. But I tried! Don't feel sorry for me. Let me tell you something . . . some of you have never known the satisfaction of doing your best in sports, the joy of excelling in class, the wonderful feeling of completing a job . . . and looking back on it knowing you have done your best. . . . I dare you to look up at the stars . . . and set your sights on one of them that you thought was unattainable.

That's a tremendous response to adversity. You tell me Clifton Cushman was not a winner that day, and a winner in life! It is your obligation as the coach to allow your players to experience this same winning attitude. Create an arena in which they can win despite the results of the game. As long as they give totally of themselves, then the game results will be incidental. The experience of being part of an all out effort will be rewarded. Ironically, this type of mindset and effort usually results in great achievement on the field. Without it, success almost never occurs.

You must create an environment in which your players become totally vulnerable. By that, I mean that they can give everything and still lose. That's scary! It's scary because it eliminates all excuses. If the other team wins despite your all-out effort, face it; they were better. There is no shame in admitting defeat to a team with superior ability. But you still are victorious – victorious in effort. You faced the challenge head on, and you didn't back down. Like Abe Lincoln,

I want my team to be able to say, "If I fail, it will be for lack of ability, and not of purpose."

Believe it or not, there have been games in my career where a team was applauded more by the fans in defeat than in victory. As a graduate of Duke University, I am always thrilled to see reference to the 1992 Duke v. University of Kentucky game as the greatest college basketball game ever played. I was listening to that game on the car radio when Christian Laettner hit the game winning shot – I almost wrecked the car. What a memory for those of us who are Blue Devil fans! But it was the reaction of the Kentucky fans that illustrates my point. Their team had lost a heart breaker, but the next day there were thousands who turned out to greet the Wildcats on their return home. The group of seniors who resurrected Kentucky basketball from a low point historically was a group of non-super stars (Jamaal Mashburn excluded). In defeat they were heralded for their tenacity and "never quit" attitude. It was this "losing" team that was embraced and nicknamed by the Kentucky faithful, as the "Unforgettables."

Despite the jaded view of many sports fans today, there is still a core of people who truly understand what the game is all about. It's all about the effort. John Stephen Akhwari was a marathon runner in the 1968 Olympic Games in Mexico City. He finished dead last. So why is he still revered and remembered? Akhwari was injured during the run. Bloodied and bandaged, Akhwari hobbled into the Olympic stadium over an hour behind the last competitor. When asked why he kept running despite the pain and the inability to win, he replied, "My country did not send me to Mexico City to start the race. They sent me here to finish." There was no upset here – or was there? For me this was an upset! It was a triumph over adversity. It, too, is "unforgettable"!

CREATE YOUR OWN CIRCUMSTANCES

The ability to create positive energy is up to each and every individual on your team. Many years ago, William Jordan wrote *The Kingship of Self-Control.* He contends that man's greatest enemy is himself: "In his weakness, man is the creature of circumstance. In his strength he is the creator of circumstance. Whether he be victim or victor depends largely upon himself." The coach's job is to guide his players to an understanding of their possibilities – an understanding that the focus is not on who they currently are as team players, but is on who they will become through hard work and dedication. Jordan states that the self-control necessary to obtain the victory is attainable "if only he will. It is but a matter of paying the price."

Will you and your players be victims of circumstance or victors? You have to teach them to see the possibilities, not the realities of their current state. Regardless of circumstance (too small, too weak, too slow) teach them how to create and become the masters of their own circumstances. Do you want your players to be quicker? If so, incorporate speed enhancement drills into your off-season and on the field conditioning. Tell them over and over that these drills, if followed diligently, will make them quicker. Find the weaknesses that inhibit individual and team success. Help each player to identify the weak point that hinders him from reaching his fullest potential. Get your players to focus on each practice as if it were their only chance to succeed and conquer those weaknesses. They must telescope their energy into that one time and place.

If you can maximize practice in this way and focus your players, the team will improve over time. That is why some teams seem to be so much better at the end of the season than at the beginning, while others seem to worsen or at best stay the same. Each player and coach must take personal responsibility over his circumstance and create his own positive one. James Allen wrote, "A man is literally what he thinks." If this is true, and I believe it to be, then your players have to think and believe in their ability to win the big games. You have to become the master of your own thoughts. Allen concludes that you must become the " . . . maker and shaper of condition, environment and destiny." If you want it badly enough, then you have to immerse yourself in the process of obtaining it. Single-mindedness and focus become the mainstays of your quest for success. This concept has application to any and all endeavors – not just football. Teach your players this simple truth, and you will teach them how to be success-ful in work, family relations, and just about everything else.

EXPOSE YOUR TEAM
TO THE BEST

For your team to play its best, your players need to model themselves on the best. I was always looking to see whom in our community and even nationally I could schedule to talk to our players before the season started or before the big game.

One year we brought in the legendary weightlifter Paul Anderson to spend a weekend with us. Paul won the Olympic heavyweight Gold Medal at the 1956 games in Melbourne, Australia. He is also the *Guinness Book of World Records* record holder for the heaviest lift ever made by a human. On June 12, 1957, Paul strapped himself into a harness and cleared 6,270 pounds in a back lift. Now that's strong! So strong that in 1992, he was named the strongest man of the century at the USA Power and Strength Symposium in Orlando, Florida.

Paul was also a great Fellowship of Christian Athletes motivational speaker. My first encounter with Paul was as a young boy. My father brought him in to speak at our church. He stayed at our house and slept in our extra slat reinforced bed (to accommodate his 450-pound frame). I also attended the Fellowship of Christian

Athletes' camp after my junior year of high school and heard him speak again. I never forgot Paul or his message. When I became a coach I always knew I wanted to bring Paul back to address my school and my team. He did just that. However, this time he came with an assistant and a Winnebago motor home.

When Paul arrived at the school, I was there to greet him. On a comical note, here was the world's strongest man standing there and directing the unloading of all of the weights that he needed for the demonstration. The assistant (a troubled ward of the courts whom Paul had rescued) and I were the only haulers. You have to remember this was the world's strongest man. He did demonstrations with 450 pounds attached to a chain and a mouthpiece. He did multiple neck raises while lifting the weights by his teeth! However, the young man and I did all of the unloading and stacking of the weights. The irony of this was not lost on my back. I was tuckered, and Paul was ready to go. For my efforts I was offered some refrigerated beef blood. I politely turned down the offer – I suddenly wasn't that thirsty.

Paul put on a memorable exhibition to our community one night, and to our school and then separately to my team the next day. But it was never the weights that he lifted that had the impact; it was what he said. Paul's theme was simple and to the point: Work hard and never quit. Believe in yourself and in each other. Don't try to take any shortcuts to success. It is only through perseverance and sheer will power that you will succeed. He also told us to never make excuses, to learn from our losses, and to do it with class by playing hard but fair. He then took out a large nail, put it in his bare hand and promptly drove it completely through a 2" x 4" piece of wood. He literally drove home his point. To this day I still have the piece of wood with the nail in it. Paul was gracious enough to autograph the wood and write "For Bruce and his team."

I admired Paul for his accomplishments, but mostly for how he lived his life. He, along with his wife, started the Paul Anderson Youth Home for troubled young men aged sixteen to twenty-one. When jail was the last alternative for these young people, Paul would take them under his wing in his home. He showed them how to win at life. Over one thousand young men under Paul's tutelage pulled off the best "upset" of all. They won the battle of life against insurmountable odds. He shared his strength and his vision with them. Paul modeled for them how to never give up no matter what. Even in his last years, while suffering from kidney disease, he never quit. It prompted one reporter to observe: "He is the world's strongest man and he also lifts weights."

Another example of "the best" for our players was Dr. Greg Shepard of "Bigger, Faster, Stronger." Dr. Shepard was at the top of my list as an inspirational and motivational speaker. I knew we needed him to help us reach the next step in our program development. We had just finished a 5-5 season. I decided that we needed someone to help inspire our team in their off-season work, so I thought it was time for the "Dr." to make a house call. Dr. Shepard agreed and flew from Utah to Delaware, where he spent an entire weekend with us and shared his vision of how to get "bigger, faster, stronger," and to reach an "11" on the effort chart.

His visit was memorable. The electricity that he generated and the knowledge that he shared was fantastic, but the next season's results were even better. We stormed back from the previous season with an undefeated regular season (10-0), an undefeated conference championship, a semi-final state championship win, and a chance to play my good friend George Glenn's team, Salesianum, in the state championship game. We lost the game 7-6, but it was a "barn-burner" right down to the last minute. Thanks to Dr. Shepard and his unique physical and mental training program, we were able to walk off the field as winners—proud of ourselves, our effort and of our season.

The confidence we gained from the "Bigger, Faster, Stronger" program and our season's success enabled us to come right back the next season. We were matched up with the reigning state champ Salesianum, the same team that had beaten us the previous year. But this year was our turn. We played a typical William Penn v. Salesianum hard fought slugfest and won the state championship game 8-0. Thanks Dr. Shepard; we will always be in your debt!

Most of our speakers, however, were local—people that our team knew and respected. Tony Glenn, a former outstanding center for the University of Delaware, was a great motivator for us. Tony is now the Executive Director of the DFRC (Delaware Foundation Reaching Citizens – with cognitive disabilities), and chairs Delaware's annual high school football All-Star Game. I asked him to speak to my team when he was still playing for the University of Delaware. Being young and still in college enabled him to relate with our players and provide inspiration and guidance both academically and athletically.

Dr. Michael Axe of First State Orthopaedics brought top-notch coaches and athletes in to speak and to inspire. Dave Tiberi, outstanding alumnus and boxer, always had a special message for us. Kevin Riley, former Philadelphia Eagle linebacker and survivor of an arm amputation, was without a doubt one of the most inspirational and memorable of our speakers as well. This is only a sampling of the type of people we invited to inspire and motivate our players. If you look hard, you too can find the people that will help you inspire and motivate your team. Many of them will be found right in your own school and community. Sometimes, it only takes a simple knock on the door: "Seek, and you will find; knock, and it will be opened to you" (Luke 11.9).

START YOUR SEASON ON A GOOD NOTE!

The Role of Music

The role of music – don't underestimate it. It is a great morale builder and motivator. Without good team morale you will not win. Napoleon once said, "Morale is to material as 3 is to1." In other words, if your opponents have great players (material) and you have great morale, morale can win it for you! If you are up against great players, you will need every edge you can get to pull off the upset. Music helps! Pick a representative group of senior players. Not all will share in the same style of music, so it is important to have a representative group to select the "upset" themes. Give suggestions, but allow them to do the choosing. Try not to interfere too much except to lay down some guidelines that include selecting music that is appropriate for school. If their selections are poor or are inappropriate, however, don't be afraid to step in. Remember, censorship is constitutionally acceptable on a football team. We live in a democracy, but in football, sometimes a benevolent dictatorship is in order.

Pick a selection of songs that mean something to the team. Ever since Rocky Balboa hit the scene in the early eighties, we have used "Eye of the Tiger," as one of our themes. We were getting ready to play in the state championship game in December of 1982. *Rocky II* had just been released. I called a local movie theater and booked a private viewing for my entire team. We went to the movie the week of our championship game. Our kids became hooked on the upset theme. They embraced the role of the "never quit" Rocky. That was when we also embraced the movie's theme song, "Eye of the Tiger," by the group Survivor. For years afterward I gave my pre-game pep talks while the *Rocky* theme was playing in the background. I would try to time what I was saying to the rhythm and volume of the song. When it hit its peak, so did the team, and we stormed out of the locker room ready to do battle.

Have you ever watched the nature channel on TV? Watch the big cats hunt their prey. Talk about focused! They never take their eyes off of the "prize." It is a one-minded, focused, intense, laser-like attack. Many times before the big game I would have my team walk past me single-file. As "The Eye of the Tiger" played in the background, I told them what I was looking for and that I'd better see it in their eyes as they walked past me. The threat was always that if I didn't see the focus in their eyes, they wouldn't play. I don't ever recall having to bench a player for not at least looking like an intensely focused "tiger."

We also used the hit song "We Are the Champions" by Queen. The song came out in October of 1977 just prior to our very first state tournament appearance under my tenure as head coach. Our team had worked hard to achieve this milestone. The lyrics, "I've paid my dues . . ." seemed to resonate with our team. Other lines from the song like " . . . bad mistakes . . . but I've come through," and "We mean to go on and on and on and on," were equally meaningful. To us it meant that no matter what happened in the game we would not quit because "We'll keep on fighting 'til the end . . . 'cause we are the champions."

We also had our own team song. Our song was written by my high school head coach and athletic director, Bill L. Cole. He took an old camp song that he knew and with some clever editing and re-arranging created our traditional team song. The song has endured since its inception in the early 1950s, and is still being sung by our teams today. The theme of the team song is that we are a team! We always work hard and we are tough. We are also a team of pals and we always stick up for each other: " . . . for every single one of us we all stick up for the rest of us." We sang this song every day at the end of practice. We sang it with enthusiasm and a harmony of spirit, though not necessarily of voices. I should note that we also sang it at the end of each and every game, win or lose. It was especially important to us when we lost a game, because the theme was about team and "sticking up" for each teammate and coach. There is no room for pointing fingers and blame when you have each other's back. Even to this day, players who played from the early fifties on still remember and can sing the team song written by Coach Cole–I know I still can! "We are the Colonials, we are the team of pals, we always work we never shirk, we are the Colonials. . . . "

I even believed that we could get inspiration from our National Anthem that was played at the beginning of every game. Instead of just going through the motions, think of the history behind the "Star Spangled Banner." Francis Scott Key wrote the song aboard ship during the 1814 British bombing of Fort McHenry in Baltimore Harbor. The song was inspired when Key caught sight of the still-standing American flag. Despite the withering attack " . . . our flag was still there." It is symbolic of great pride and a "never quit" attitude. No matter what, we will endure. That's just how I wanted our team to approach the game – with pride and a "never quit" resolve.

"America the Beautiful" is another classic that fit our philosophy. It talks of "brotherhood," "stern impassioned stress" (focused and passionate play), "self control," and doing something for "more than self."

How about the "Marines' Hymn," – the oldest official song in the United States Military – and its line, "We have fought in every clime and place . . ."? I always told our team that we had to be prepared mentally and physically to play any time, any place, and under any conditions. Night or day, rain or shine, would never be our concern. We would be ready – just like the Marines! So, write your own song, borrow from the ones I have mentioned here, or pick your own tunes. But don't overlook the power of music, because music may "soothe the savage breast," but it fires up the teenage soul!

The Role of Movies

I have already mentioned the *Rocky II* movie, a great one to watch together as a team. After watching that movie together, our team felt as though it could conquer the world. Another favorite is *Remember The Titans*, released in 2000. This film was based on the actual 1971 season of the T. C. Williams High School in Alexandria, Virginia. Although Denzel Washington and Will Patton are the stars of the film, the actual stars were the two real coaches, Herman Boone and Bill Yoast. I had the pleasure of meeting these two fine men and hearing in person their accounts of that remarkable season. For us the theme of the movie is brotherhood – team as family. Hard work, discipline, and unselfishness win games and bonds individuals into a team. The book and the movie are inspirational for any and all. The music score and sound track to this movie are also exceptional, especially the main track, "Titan Spirit." I still hear that selection being used on many televised football games.

Rudy, released in 1993, has to rank right up there with the best of the football movies. It is about indomitable spirit and sacrifice. It is particularly good for all non-starting athletes on your team to watch. Part of the message is that no matter what his position or your spot on the depth chart, every player has an important role and a contribution to make to the team. No one can watch *Rudy* and not be emotionally moved by that story.

There are many other movies that are great for teams to watch. Old classics such as the 1940 movie *Knute Rockne: All American,* and more modern ones, like *Friday Night Lights,* and *Invincible* (the Vince Papale story) can be used as motivational tools for your team. But a coach has to be careful to select only those movies that are appropriate. Some of today's films have some good content but seem to be more interested in the sensational aspects of sports. I always avoided those movies. For me, they have no place in a program that espouses positive roles and positive images. I would only recommend movies that enhanced our goals and our philosophy: Give it your all, never quit, and do it the right way.

If Hollywood movies aren't your thing, don't forget the vast storehouse of great instructional and motivational videos or CDs. There are too many of these to name, but let me share a few of my favorites with you: The *NFL's Greatest Hits, The NFL's Greatest Tackles, Great Moments in College Football,* and any and all motivational videos that Dr. Greg Shepard produces with "Bigger, Faster, Stronger." You can show these to your entire team or loan them out to individual players for overnight watching. Our players really enjoyed these videos and asked to watch them often. Whatever you do, don't neglect the media of music and movies/videos. They will become indispensable tools for you to help inspire and motivate your team.

ALUMNI NIGHT – TRADITION

One of the best ideas we used at our school was the Alumni Night. Before our big rivalry game we would bring in our past alumni. We always tried to represent someone from each decade. We started with our legendary Delaware Hall of Fame and University of Delaware Hall of Fame coach, Bill L. Cole. He represented the late forties and fifties and a stellar 25-year head-coaching reign ending in 1973. We followed him up with John Hopkins Sr., Jake Ryan, and Jimmy Trabaudo, who along with Johnny Lane were part of our school's fabled "Four J's" backfield that cranked out thirty-three victories in a row in the early fifties. They were players on the teams that established our school as one of the elite football teams in the state–they won our school's first unofficial state championship (the official state championship format in our state was not established until the early 1970s). They also established some of the early "upsets" that became the lore that I grew up on as a young kid, one of many young men who aspired to someday play for the William Penn Colonial football team and Coach Bill Cole.

Bob Tattersall (a 230-plus game career winning coach, and still going strong), who played in the latter half of the fifties came next, followed by Jim Gregg (undefeated 1962 team), and many of my old teammates of the mid-sixties like Buddy Hewes, Fred Kern, and Rick Till. Jim Linus of the late sixties, now a local sporting goods representative, would speak next. He was followed by representatives of our teams from the seventies: Jim Hopkins (still coaching football and track at our school), Jimmy Sherman (current head baseball coach at the University of Delaware), and John Behornar, (a local youth coach and firefighter).

The 1980s were represented by our current head coach, Bill C. Cole, who played on our first Division I state championship team in 1982. A multitude of players from the later 80s, 90s and 2000s, also took part, along with our current recent graduates. Former players Jim Hopkins, Paul Robinson, Tom Cole, Drew Moffett, Erik Jones, Matt Brainard, Tom Fleming, John Taggart, Ken Buchanan, Bo Hunter, Jeff Hewes, Carl Eaton, Rich Bryson, and Bret Vendrick not only spoke, but have come back to coach at our school. There were too many who participated over the years to name each individually; but not too many to remember each one's unique contribution to our success.

Each one would get up in front of our team at a pizza dinner (supplied by our Booster Club) and recount their stories of playing our archrival. The current players always listened attentively and soaked up almost sixty years of the tradition of our team's past performances in the big game. We seemed to come out especially fired up the next day when we played the game. I always invited the special guests to accompany us before the game and at halftime to the locker room to help motivate us. They didn't have to say anything–their presence said it all.

Your team must be focused on the present; however, it's amazing how visions of the past affected our enthusiasm and desire to play today in the present. It wasn't a gimmick! It was a genuinely enjoyable evening together with old and young sharing a common bond. The past players took a renewed interest in their old school and the current crop of players. Both groups found it easy to relate. We transcended time when we talked about the game. I even got into the act and was able to relive my senior year when we upset our previously undefeated rival. It was as if time stood still. The years have never erased the memories for me. The only thing that has changed is the fact that the older I get, the better I was! I always came out of that meeting (bad knees and all) ready to play. The body might not have responded properly, but the heart was ready to go.

ACRES OF DIAMONDS

There is one critical secret to success. The secret is that there is no secret. It is there for all to find. It is a "blueprint" instead – a methodology of persistence, sacrifice and hard work. Too many people try to find shortcuts and disregard the fact that if they had just stayed focused on their goal and worked hard they probably would have found the elusive success for which they were searching. A story told to me by my father, Dr. Brooks E. Reynolds, will help illustrate the point.

My father was a Methodist minister. He and my mother graduated from Temple University in Philadelphia, Pennsylvania. It was there that he discovered the writings of the founder of Temple University, Russell H. Conwell. Conwell wrote a "gem" of a book entitled *Acres of Diamonds*. My father preached many sermons on Conwell's parable and used it as a model to develop and grow small churches into thriving ones. I heard the story so many times that I incorporated it and applied it to just about every facet of my life and career.

In the book, Conwell relates the story of an excursion down the Tigris River, led by an Arab guide. The guide had many tales to tell during the trip, but there was one special story that he reserved for his "particular friends." In this story, a wealthy Persian farmer named Ali Hafed was one day visited by a priest. After recounting the creation of the world to Hafed, the priest told him that diamonds are the highest of God's mineral creations. If Ali Hafed had just "one diamond the size of his thumb, he could purchase the whole country. If he had a mine of diamonds, he could place his children upon the thrones of countries throughout the world." Ali was no longer contented with what he had; he had to have more – he had to have a diamond mine. He asked the priest where he could find the diamonds. The priest told him that all he had to do was to "go and find them." Ali Hafed sold his farm, left his family, and began his search for the coveted diamonds. His fruitless search left him in poor health and poverty-stricken. In despair, he finally ended his own life.

One day, the man who had purchased Ali Hafed's farm was watering his camel in the garden located on his property. He saw a black pebble that reflected a brilliant ray of light and a panorama of hues that made up all the colors of the rainbow. The man did not know it was a diamond, but when the priest came by to visit and noticed the pebble on the mantel in the man's home, he immediately knew what it was and inquired where it had been found. The man took the priest out to the garden, and there they discovered more. The old Arab guide concluded, "Thus was discovered the diamond mine of Golcanda . . . the most magnificent diamond mine in the history of mankind. . . . The Kohinoor and the Orloff diamonds, belonging to the crown jewels of England and Russia (the largest diamonds on earth) came from that mine."

The moral of this story is simple: had Ali Hafed stayed home, he would have had "Acres of Diamonds." His treasure was right in his own back yard! When I apply this to coaching, the implications are clear. If you want to be successful, don't envy others, don't make excuses, and work hard with what you've got. Too many coaches complain that their players are not as big or fast or as strong as their opponents. Their school is too small and they don't have the facilities and equipment to compete. If only they had this or that they could win. The excuses are numerous and interchangeable, but they are equally self-defeating. Make no excuses! Get to work! Mine the diamonds in your own garden.

THE IMPORTANCE OF YOUR STAFF

The book *Acres of Diamonds* has a clear message. The grass is *not* always greener on the other side of the fence. Look in your own backyard for the help you need to achieve your goals. Work with your own players and make them the best that they can be. Lead your staff in helping your players achieve their highest potential – for both the individual players and the team.

No man is an island – how true! A staff of assistants with diverse talents working towards the same goal is essential. There is no doubt that without our assistant coaches' individual and collective contributions, our team would never have reached the level of success that we enjoyed. Each coach had his own personal strengths and unique character that allowed us to work in harmony for one goal: to win the right way. For us, winning the right way meant to do it with character and class by exhibiting the highest standard of sportsmanship. Each assistant was first and foremost a great teacher. If I had to make a choice between a person who knew football vs. a great teacher who knew nothing about football, I would choose the great teacher every time. You can teach a person how to coach football, but you can't always make a person a great teacher. It's all about communication, and my assistants were the best.

I hope that in looking back on our career together, our coaches would say that they had a vested interest in our success partly because they had a voice in our decision-making; their contributions were always appreciated. I tried to create a climate wherein my assistants had an opportunity to be "heard" and not just an opportunity to "have their say." Jim Collins, in his book *Good to Great,* sums up this philosophy of leadership. He talks about the need for a leader to create a climate where "the truth is heard and the brutal facts confronted." You don't want to have "yes" men as your assistants. They should be independent thinkers who are willing to state their opinions. They need freedom to make suggestions that will improve your program, and they need to feel that they can tell you when you are wrong. You need to be able to accept what they are saying. You may not always agree, and that is fine, but you must listen to what they say and evaluate it on its merit. You can't just tune their input out.

My philosophy was simple. I did most of the things I did with our program because I had a good reason. If an assistant could show me a better way, I would change it—but he had to prove to me that it was a better way.

My staff and I sometimes disagreed on how to approach a game or what plays to use. From time to time a coach would make a suggestion that I just didn't agree with. I do know that I weighed each and every suggestion carefully. I had an offensive, defensive and kicking game system etched solidly in my mind —I knew it, the coaches knew it and the players knew it. We also knew how to execute the system.

From time to time one of the coaches would tell me that we needed a new play for a particular opponent or a new defensive scheme. I was usually hesitant and said, "No," to the first request. Coach Bill Legge often joked about how he hounded me for weeks and weeks to put in some special passing schemes. For me the timing was just not right. I had to see how it would fit into our overall offensive scheme. Our system was one that had each play complementing or setting up another. I never liked a grab-bag approach. Bill, however, diligently kept at it and finally won me over. He knew that his idea had merit and that it would fit into our scheme. He was right. We used the new passing schemes, and they brought us immediate success. They became an integral part of our offense. I feel that I had that relationship with all of my staff. I hope that they all can say upon reflection that I was always receptive to their suggestions even if I disagreed.

In dealing with suggested changes, I took a page out of the book from my high school coach and athletic director, Bill Cole. (I might add that Jack Holloway and Bill Legge, who followed Bill as athletic director, have read the same book.) As athletic director, Coach Cole ran a solid and tight fiscally responsible program. Many of us would go to him and ask for something special for our program. Bill would often initially say no. He later shared that his thinking was that if we really wanted something and it had merit, we would ask again. Often on the second request, he would say yes. With Bill, you always got what you *needed*, not necessarily everything you *wanted*. If it would be good for your program and our school, he was first in line to make sure you got it. But you had to prove to Bill that it had merit.

Conversely, I held strongly to the things that I knew worked best for our team. Sometimes as the head coach you have to say no to requests for change. Change for the sake of change was never a priority of mine.

I think the types of relationships that we built between our staff members developed trust in each other and forged loyalty. There is nothing worse than losing a game and hearing staff members criticize the play-calling or decision-making of the head coach. It is a cancer. It will spread and consume you, your staff, and your team. You can disagree behind closed doors, but when the door is opened you have to emerge as a united front. Thank goodness I was blessed with a staff that was talented and independent-thinking, but also team-oriented and loyal! I sincerely owe whatever success I had as a head coach to them and, of course, to those we coached.

Loyalty is also a critical factor in developing the climate for the upset. In fact, it is a must. As I have mentioned already, I was blessed with a very talented group of assistant coaches. They were truly outstanding coaches, but most importantly they were loyal. Remember, though, loyalty is a two-way street. You have to exhibit the same measure of loyalty to your assistants that you demand of them.

One of the best stories I ever heard abut loyalty I got from legendary coach Grant Teaff at a 1972 football coaches' convention in Atlantic City. At the time, he was head coach of the Baylor University Bears. Coach Teaff is currently the Executive Director of the American Football Coaches Association. I give Coach Teaff the credit for this story, but it is really an apocryphal story, passed from one coach to another over the years. I am going to tell it the modified and embellished way I have been telling it at speaking engagements, with the blessing of all participants, for over 35 years and counting. Feel free to adapt it for your own situation!

In my second year as a rookie coach, my team won all of our games but nine. (Re-read that last sentence. That's a trick I learned early in my career. How you say something can make a huge difference. It sounds like we did great! I like it a lot better than saying we lost 9 games and only won 1 game that year.) The season was over, and my assistant coach Howdy Duncan (an avid hunter) had been bugging me for years to go hunting with him someday. I am not a hunter. I always said "No"; however, in a weak moment I finally agreed. We had a longtime die-hard fan named Ken Short. He was a Booster member who owned a large farm in Sussex County, Delaware. He had always told me that if I ever wanted to hunt, he would love for me to use his land. I always had said, "Thanks, but no thanks." I told Howdy about the offer and we agreed to go down and see if we could hunt on his property.

On the way to the farm in Howdy's pickup, well supplied with guns, ammo, decoys, and food prepared by his wife Karen, I told Howdy that I was nervous about the reception that we might get. I hadn't seen Ken at our weekly Booster meetings for quite a while. Had the mounting losses soured him on me as a coach? Loyal Howdy told me that if Ken said anything negative to me, just let him know—he'd take care of it. Howdy was a rough and tumble guy that didn't take any grief from anyone. For that reason, I told him that when we got there I wanted him to stay in the truck and let me talk to the man alone. I didn't want Howdy over-reacting and causing a problem.

When we got there, I went up to the door and knocked. Ken came to the door with the longest face I had ever seen. I glanced back at Howdy, who was watching intently. Ken greeted me as I explained to him that I would like to take him up on his offer to hunt on his farm. He said absolutely, it would be his pleasure. He even invited Howdy and me to stay for dinner that evening. I declined, but thanked him and said, "If I can ever do anything for you, just let me know."

Bruce Reynolds

Ken said, "Coach, I hate to ask, but I really don't have anyone else who can help me. Do you see that scrawny, sickly [you could count every rib] mule over there by your truck? Well, that mule is my son Charles' pet mule. He's had him ever since he was ten. He's away at school and doesn't know his mule is near death. The vet said that he would put him down. But Coach, the vet bill is already sky-high and my wife Mary Jane won't let me do it. Would you please shoot the mule?"

"Whoa, no!" I said. "I can't shoot your mule!"

He said, "Coach, I won't ask you again." And then with a sigh and a tear in his eye he added, "But you'll never know how much it would mean to me if you would."

I couldn't believe it, but after much anguish, I finally said, "OK, I'll do it!" As I started to go back to the truck, I know that Ken's face and mine were as long and dour as the sick mule's face.

When I got into the truck, Howdy demanded, "What did he say?" I told him that Ken had told me that I was the sorriest excuse he had ever seen as a coach! If they fired me yesterday it wouldn't be soon enough!

I then said to Howdy, "I'm so mad, I can't see straight!" I took the gun down from the rack, loaded the ammo and rolled down the window.

Howdy screamed, "What're you doing?"

I said, "I'm so mad, I'm going to shoot his mule!" While Howdy was yelling, I took dead aim and shot the mule. Before I could turn around to tell Howdy the truth, I heard a thunderous "Boom, boom!" I jumped around toward Howdy and yelled, "What have you done?" He yelled back, "I just shot his cow; let's get out of here!"

Now that's loyalty. Thanks to Grant Teaff for a great storyline.

All kidding aside, you have to have that kind of loyalty to weather the storms of coaching. I could not have lasted 27 years as a head coach without it.

I have one last comment on staff. Be sure to put good coaches in charge of your younger players. We were fortunate enough to have a junior varsity and a freshman program. I placed exceptional coaches in the positions of head and assistant coaches for these teams. I had started my career as a freshman coach and saw the value and importance of those positions. Outstanding people like Richard Farmer (Rich later became a principal and now serves as vice president of our State Board of Education); Jim Tosi (Jim later became a superb head coach, taking his team to the state finals); Jim Hopkins (former player and head track coach at our school); our current varsity head coach, Bill C. Cole (Bill played on our first State Championship team in 1982); Steve Lepre (now varsity defensive coordinator in addition to long-time stints coaching baseball and basketball); and Dave Taylor served in these capacities. Dave Taylor and I started our coaching careers together in 1971. From 1974 to 2000, in addition to his varsity duties, Dave served as my JV head coach.

I truly believe that our success at the varsity level was directly related to the super job that these coaches did at the JV and freshman level. Bill C. Cole served many years as our head freshman coach before he took over the reigns as our head varsity coach. I know that the experience of being the head freshman coach honed his coaching, organizational, and administrative skills to the point that when he took over the entire program as the head coach, the transition was flawless. He already has a state championship and several conference championships under his belt with, I'm sure, many more to come.

TEAM DOCTOR AND TRAINER

The role of the team medical doctor and the team trainer are often overlooked. We were blessed at my school. Dr. Charles Wagner was our team physician for over 40 years. He was a local family physician with a keen interest in sports medicine. "Doc" was way ahead of his time in that area. He also loved our school and our athletes. From the team physicals in August to the last game of the season, he was always there for our team. Doc Wagner knew when an athlete was injured and should not play; and just as important, he understood the bumps and bruises of football. He knew when an athlete, with proper rehabilitation, could return to play. We never jeopardized the future health of our players, and Dr. Wagner was the major factor in that decision.

It was a sad day when Doc Wagner retired, but we were again fortunate to have Dr. Michael Axe and First State Orthopaedics come to the rescue. His medical group paved the way for providing great medical expertise and coverage not only to our teams, but also to many of the sports teams in our county and our state. Dr. Axe was responsible for bringing one of our former outstanding players, Dr. Michael Conway, back into our program. Mike shared the same values as Dr. Wagner and we benefited immensely from his skill and commitment to his old team.

Our team trainer shared the same responsibility for our team's well being. I know how important the trainer is to the team because I spent the early part of my career without one. What a relief to have our athletes attended to by a trained physical therapist and trainer! Our trainers performed their duties on a day-to-day basis. The knowledge gained from working with the athletes every day is important. We were blessed with outstanding trainers throughout my career. Paul Schweizer was our first trainer, and he was a gem. He was a former outstanding player at the University of Delaware. He understood sports medicine, and he also understood athletes and the game of football. He was tough, but caring. That is the perfect fit for a trainer.

The trainers who followed Paul were in his image and did a great job for us. Rudy Rudawsky and Vinnie Ranalli provided us with their expertise, their compassion, and their commitment to our team. Rudy Rudawsky went on to work with the United States men's soccer team, and Vinnie is still working his magic with our athletes at William Penn.

All our trainers were very committed people who played an integral part in our success. Paul Schweizer, as I mentioned, was our first trainer. Paul and I developed a strong and lasting friendship based on our mutual love of the game and how it should be played. Paul had an intensity and passion that was infectious. He never did anything halfway. With Paul, there was only one way to do anything–full throttle ahead.

Paul initiated a special program that he called the "Beef Patrol." The Beef Patrol consisted of approximately six of our largest players who needed to trim down and improve their speed, strength and quickness. One of Paul's great success stories involved an unforgettable player of ours named "Big Al." Big Al was a 405 pound, 6'5" tackle. The first challenge was to determine Big Al's true weight, as our scales only went up to 350 pounds. I called my friend Aaron Miller of Miller's Meat Market and asked him if he had a scale big enough to weigh Big Al. He said of course, we could use his meat scale at the store. I took Big Al to Miller's Market and introduced him to Aaron. Aaron placed Big Al on a hook attached to a steel cable on the scale. Big Al had to perch on the hook while hanging onto the steel cord until Aaron could calibrate the scale and get the reading. The scale read 405 pounds.

There was an opening to the room that was visible from the meat counter. Several women were looking at the meat display when they noticed Big Al hanging from the meat hook. Aaron and I got the biggest kick out of that. I don't know what the women were thinking, but I do know they didn't purchase any meat that day!

That's when Paul Schweizer and the Beef Patrol began their work. I don't know how he did it, but Paul was able to put Big Al on the starting line the next season at 333 pounds. He looked like an NFL lineman. Big Al was now a force to be reckoned with. I give Paul the credit for this, but also give Al credit for having the courage and perseverance to accomplish this amazing transformation. Paul showed him the vision of what he could be, made him believe in it, and Big Al accomplished it!

Rudy Rudawsky was our next trainer. Rudy later became the United States men's soccer team trainer. He is given credit for possibly saving the life of the United States' midfielder Tab Ramos during the World Cup Games in 1994. Ramos had just taken a savage elbow to the head by Brazil's Leonardo. Rudy responded quickly and directed the care of Ramos immediately. Ramos was rushed to a hospital where it was discovered that a life-threatening skull fracture had occurred. Without the proper procedures and immediate on field attention by Rudy, Ramos' life may have been on the line.

Vinnie Ranalli was the last trainer with whom I had the privilege to work. Vinnie was a former outstanding high school quarterback. He is now our school district's full-time trainer, and works with all of our district athletes. He earned this position because of his outstanding character and work ethic. He also has a special knack of being able to relate to the players. Like Paul, he has played and knows what it takes to play this game.

All of our trainers were able to keep our athletes on the field, and if they were injured, they got them back on the field quickly. I must add that getting them back quickly was never done at the risk of harm to the student-athletes. We developed the policy that we would never put a player back on the field unless the following criteria were met: (1) the player said he was healthy and ready to go; (2) the parent or guardian gave approval; (3) the personal or team doctor gave approval; and (4) the trainer gave his stamp of approval. Following this procedure gave all involved the peace of mind that our players were healthy and ready to compete. If you truly want to win the big game, don't overlook the importance of a good trainer and team doctor. You can't win with your players on the sideline. When you need them for the game they'll be healthy and ready to go.

I can't conclude a discussion of trainers without mentioning Carl Eaton. Carl was a starting guard and linebacker, as well as co-captain, for our 1992 team. Sidelined by a preseason knee injury, he stayed with the team as an unofficial "student coach" and was a major contributor to the team's success in winning the state championship that year. When Carl began his college studies at the University of Delaware to become a physical therapist and trainer, I knew great things were to come for him. Carl came back to William Penn and helped coach our team while working with Paul Schweizer and Pro Physical Therapy. Carl then did a stint as a trainer at the University of Delaware. His growing stature in the physical training field eventually garnered a job with the Indiana Pacers of the National Basketball Association. In an article by outstanding sports writer Kevin Tresolini of the Wilmington, Delaware *News Journal* (June 18, 2007), there appeared a comment by the Pacers six-time all-star, Jermaine O'Neal: "I've been pain-free pretty much this year, and I attribute this to Carl." He added, "A lot of people say it's the best all-around year of my career."

I tell you these brief stories about my experiences with our trainers to underscore my belief that you will not be successful without the assistance of a good team doctor and athletic trainer. They truly are critical components to your team's success and the pursuit of the upset.

PARENTS

One of the most-neglected aspects of many programs is the role of the parents. Too often, parents are regarded primarily as fund raisers and second-guessers, but as a coach you can never underestimate the value of having a group of committed and loyal parents/guardians. You only have your players an average of four seasons for approximately two hours a day during the season. Their parents have been with them for a lifetime. For twenty-seven football seasons, I met with my players' parents and other Booster members every Tuesday night. I inherited this tradition from my high school coach and mentor Billy Cole. Starting in the 1940s, Billy was the first coach in the state of Delaware to film his games and to take his players to a one-week pre-season camp. He also was our state's first All-Star game coach and helped found our Blue Hen Conference. He was a University of Delaware All-American halfback and has been enshrined in the Delaware Hall of Fame. I had the great fortune of playing for him while in high school and working for him prior to following in his footsteps as the head coach. They were huge shoes to fill, but with his help, the transition was smooth. One important lesson I learned from Billy was to put myself on the block every Tuesday and work with the parents directly.

Sometimes it is uncomfortable to have to deal directly with parents, but the pros far outweigh the cons. It enables you to convey and reinforce your program's philosophy on a weekly basis. It also gives parents the opportunity to talk with the head coach concerning their son and his role in your program. I feel the parents appreciated the opportunity to have this frequent direct communication link with the coach. You can minimize and often eliminate parental negativity by dealing with the problems every week and not letting them smolder and fester un-addressed.

We played our freshman games on Thursdays, our varsity games on Friday night or Saturday afternoons, and our JV games after school on Mondays. Tuesday night was the ideal time to show the parents the film of the previous week's varsity game. We later expanded this by adding two more stations where we could show JV and freshman parents their sons' games as well. We included a quick scouting report on our upcoming opponent and talked about some of the things we would have to focus on to win the next game. I felt this component of our meeting went a long way in making our parents and Boosters feel a part of the team.

We shared our goals and our dreams together. We never talked about personnel, however. Nor were negative comments ever permitted regarding any of the players. Only general areas for improvement were up for discussion if we were not playing well. Our goal was to promote our team concept and talk about the positive steps our team was taking to improve our play. Everyone understood the rules, and over the years, only a few lost sight of our goals of harmony, loyalty, sportsmanship and positive reinforcement in the molding of young men into a unified team.

When you are preparing for the "big game" don't forget the parents. Include them in your preparation. Share with them your vision for the win. Enlist their aid in getting their sons ready. Ask them to help you keep their players focused that week on the game. Tell them that their sons must zero in on the life priorities: faith, family, and schoolwork. Everything else that week must be channeled in on the game. Time with the girlfriend, long talks on the phone, protracted video game sessions, hanging out at the mall, and any other distraction must be put aside. Don't get me wrong—the above priorities should be stressed every day of the year; however, this week is special. To achieve the upset, a laser-sharp focus must be obtained.

One technique that I used from time to time was the personal letter. I would address the letter to the player's parents. The letter would be a solicitation for them to aid us in preparing their son for the big game. The letter would address starters, substitutes and injured players alike. Everyone's role would be covered in the letter. They would be reminded that their son's contribution, whatever his position or status, would be critical that week. What each player brought to the practice field would ultimately dictate the outcome of the game. The letter stressed the above-mentioned priorities along with pointers on nutrition and proper rest. Again, this is nothing different than what is preached all year long; however, the emphasis at this particular time has an incredible effect on the players. When a young man is sufficiently motivated, and his parents are behind him one hundred percent, your chances of pulling off the upset will rise exponentially.

Not every player on your team has parents or guardians who are supportive, but most have someone in their life that they look up to. Find that person and enlist him or her in the preparation for the upset. You are generating positive ions that miraculously flow from one person to another and multiply the excitement and the confidence of your players. It's like compound interest at the bank. I can't explain it, but it works!

SUPPORT FROM THE
SCHOOL COMMUNITY

In addition to your parent Booster organization, don't overlook the other organized school groups and game day co-participants. Never underestimate the role of the cheerleaders, the band and the band-front groups. They share the field with you and can be instrumental in your success.

Early in my career I started what I called the "Launch the Season Party," held the night before the last pre-season scrimmage. The cheerleaders, band, and band-front groups watched us play each week, and we appreciated tremendously their support. However, we never got to watch them perform. So, at the Launch the Season Party each group performed its routine before a cheering and enthusiastic football team. The cheerleaders (varsity and JV), followed by the flag twirlers and the rifle group, performed and received our special attention and appreciation. I felt that it helped to create a bond between the team and the other performing groups. We were one school, one team—"All for one and one for all."

We also honored our senior players and had them present a red rose to the senior cheerleaders and band-front members. This "Rose Ceremony" always had special meaning for us and the young ladies who received the roses. We ended the evening with the entire team singing our team song. If we had a new assistant coach, "tradition" said that he had to sing the team song as a soloist. Whenever we had a particularly bad singer we would try to help him out. But to tell you the truth, I always liked to see the coaches struggle with it all by themselves–I think my motivation for this had something to do with overcoming adversity.

OTHER MAJOR CONTRIBUTORS

Zig Ziglar, in *See You at the Top*, states, "The world has a way, not only of stepping aside for men and women who know where they are going, but it often joins and helps them reach their objective." How true! I have personally benefited my entire career from the volunteers in our program that wanted to be a part of our vision. They clearly understood our goal, and they volunteered their time and their expertise in the areas that could benefit us the most. Our volunteers were an integral part of our success. As a matter of fact, I don't know how we would have reached our level of success without each and every one of them.

Let me run down a list of just a few of these major contributors to our program. From our school I have already mentioned Neale Clopper, who worked with me and then took sole responsibility for our weight room—I will always be in his debt for his unselfish service and friendship. Jack Carney became our football guidance counselor and coordinated our college recruiting efforts. Because of his dedicated work, our student-athletes were always given the best information, exposure, and opportunity to continue their playing days and their education at the collegiate level. Jack and I put together a college recruiting manual to guide our players and their parents through the maze of information surrounding scholarships, admission and college selection. Joel Schlicter (English teacher/tennis coach) became the long-time press box announcer of William Penn football games. John Hopkins served as the head of our sideline "chain gang crew" for my entire 27 years as the head coach. Dr. Charles W. Wagner was our team physician for forty years (talk about devotion). Dr. Michael Axe coordinated our team care after Dr. Wagner retired. Dr. Michael Conway (a former football and wrestling standout at our school) continued our outstanding physician care. Our succession of trainers – Paul Schweizer, Rudy Rudawsky, and Vinnie Ranalli–kept our players healthy and on the field. Good friend Paul Lanouette ("Paulie" to me) cooked more hot dogs in our concession stand than anyone could ever remember or count. Not to be left out are Booster presidents Sandy Dwyer, Paul Lanouette, Pete Faverio, Harry Moffett, and many other great and dedicated Booster Club officers and members whose support cannot be measured adequately. Bill Cole, Jack Holloway and Bill Legge have served (in that order) with uncommon leadership and devotion as our school's athletic directors (almost 60 years of combined service). The support of school district superintendents Ray Christian and Dr. George Meney (along with our Board of Education), was also invaluable to our success.

Community members also contributed their talents and time. The Fred Brown family was a coach's gift from heaven. Fred Brown was our videographer. Fred later turned over the duties to his children – Kathy, Gerald, and Eric. Toward the end of my career the two boys filmed every game, and Kathy took over as our game photographer. Collectively the Brown family filmed our games for my entire career. What a tremendous asset they were to our game analysis and preparation each week!

I have saved Harold Hoagland for last, because as a sports reporter he always got the last word! Harold has been our team historian since the dawn of history (well, almost). "Hoag," as he is affectionately called, established a strong sense of school tradition in the wider community through his writing for the local town newspaper. He personally has seen and covered more William Penn sporting events than anyone alive.

The list could go on and on, but hopefully you get the point. The key to program success and the key to the upset lie within each and every one of the people in your program. I owe a deep and personal debt to these friends for their unselfish contributions. Each person involved was a key contributor to our program. Coaches, find these people, ask them to help, give them a job, and then turn them loose! Find the people in your own community who will put their shoulder to the harness and pull right alongside of you and your program. You need them—you can't do it alone. Seek them out and they will embrace you and the team. Their support will take your team to heights not imagined. That's exactly what happened with our program. We benefited immensely from the members of our community and their vocal and physical support. They caught our vision and wanted to be a part of it. You won't have to look far to find them. These key people can be found right in your own backyard – "Acres of Diamonds."

HARRY KUTCH:
Teacher and Coach

The importance of the influence of teachers, coaches, and other adults often will not be evident for many years. As a case in point, my own high school basketball coach and math teacher, Harry Kutch, had a profound effect on my development as a future coach and as a person. Harry was named Teacher of the Year for the state of Delaware in 1998. Speaking on his behalf at the state Department of Education Teacher of the Year Banquet, I shared these facts to demonstrate just what an impact his teaching and coaching had on me: "He taught me math – I became a history teacher. He coached me in varsity basketball–I went to Duke on a football scholarship." But all joking aside, his influence was truly significant.

Coach Kutch was always preaching to us to do the right thing. We had team rules, but the basic rule was clear: We all know the difference between right and wrong – so we should do the right thing. How would our actions reflect on us, our parents, our school and our team? If our actions would reflect negatively, then don't do it. It was that simple.

Harry himself is a fierce competitor – I found that out in our weekly faculty basketball skirmishes. He coached with the same intensity. One of the things I admired most was his demeanor on and off the court. Win or lose, he always came back to practice the next day with new resolve, high spirits, and his great sense of humor. But most of all I enjoyed and benefited from the life-lessons he taught us when I played for him on the school basketball team.

One night before a game I went into the locker room and saw that someone had written some objectionable graffiti on our team blackboard. I was the only one in the room at the time. I went over and erased the board. What I didn't know was that Coach Kutch had also seen it. He had left it up to see if anyone on his team would take the responsibility to erase it. Who would do the right thing? When we gathered for the pre-game talk, he inquired as to who had erased the board. I told him that I had. He told me in front of the team that he was proud of me. In that one moment, those simple words, "I'm proud of you," meant the world to me. His statement reinforced in my mind that doing the right thing is important. It also reinforced Coach Kutch's point that doing the right thing when no one else is looking is the ultimate test.

This incident may seem trivial to many, but I know what it meant to me. It endeared my coach to me and created a life-long friendship as well as a commitment to try always to do the right thing. Coaches, you may never know the impact of a few kind words spoken to an impressionable young player. Long after you have forgotten, your players will still remember and be influenced by your words and actions. As Mother Teresa once said, "Kind words can be short and easy to speak, but their echoes are truly endless." So choose your words carefully. You are in a position to mold the character of young lives. As John Wooden of UCLA says in his book *They Call Me Coach*, "Be more concerned with your character than with your reputation, because your character is who you really are, while your reputation is merely what others think you are."

A COACH'S COACHES

Charles T. Jones writes, "You are today the same you [sic] will be five years from now, except for two things: the people you meet and the books you read." I took this to heart early in my coaching career. I literally read everything I could get my hands on regarding football and coaching. I also met and was influenced by some outstanding individuals early in my coaching career. Aside from my own staff, two people stand out. When I was just starting out I met a young coach who had a profound effect on me. His name was Tom Olivadotti of Salesianum School in Wilmington, Delaware. Tom went on to enjoy an outstanding collegiate and NFL career. He was the defensive coordinator for the 1983 University of Miami National Champions under head coach Howard Schnellenberger. From there he moved to the NFL, where he spent twenty years with the Cleveland Browns, Miami Dolphins, Minnesota Vikings, New York Giants, and the Houston Texans. During his tenure with the Dolphins, Tom served as Don Shula's defensive coordinator.

Tom had a major influence on my development of a personal "style" of coaching. He told me that I should establish a system of offense, defense and kicking game that suited my personal style and

71

my type of players. He told me that I had to master my own system, but to read and research other systems of play. It was important to know what was out there. By becoming an expert on other systems and styles of play, Tom felt that any coach could better prepare himself and his team for any eventuality. If someone tried to surprise him with a change-up defense or offense, he would be mentally prepared. Tom knew the strengths and weaknesses of each and every system. They could throw the "kitchen sink" at Tom and he would have an answer.

Fortunately, I listened to him. My coaches and I always went into each game with a plan to attack or defend against what our scouts told us to expect. We also practiced against all possible situations that could be presented to us. You can't do this at the last minute, however. You have to start the first week of practice. For example, when we started teaching our base defense in early summer practice, we would also cover the adjustments to every possible formation we could encounter. If someone split, flanked, or slotted receivers, we taught the adjustment from our base defense. If a team went unbalanced, or end-over unbalanced, we taught how to automatically adjust. We went so far as to teach how to adjust to both tackles and guards split to one side or the other, leaving only a center on the ball.

Some may view this as a waste of time, but in the course of my career we actually encountered all of these situations and more. In each case we were able to adjust with confidence and a minimum of confusion. So coaches, take heed of Charles T. Jones and Tom Olivadotti, and read everything you can get your hands on regarding your sport. You never know when you will need to call on that storehouse of knowledge.

In 1975, Tom also introduced me to his superb high school assistant coach, George Glenn. When Tom left to coach at Princeton,

George took over the reigns as the head coach of Salesianum School. George and I developed a friendship and bond that still exists today. Together we have battled each other on the gridiron, started a football camp ("Blue Chip Camp"–still going strong), and shared our coaching philosophies, personal life triumphs, and disappointments. When I was most in need, George was there. I hope he feels the same way. To say that George had a tremendous impact on me as a person and as a coach would be an understatement.

George has always been "the best" at precise and exhaustive game preparation. He was a true coaching nemesis for us. He had the uncanny ability to infuse into his players the same passion that he had for the game. When we had to play his team, we knew that we would have to go against an impassioned team that was thoroughly prepared to take our heads off! The great thing about our games, however, was the camaraderie and the sportsmanship that was always displayed. We were mortal football enemies on the field, but we were friends at the same time. We played our games with great pride and with great respect for each other. I know that I was elated when we won, but genuinely disappointed for George and his team at the same time. I also know that when we lost, I was disappointed for my team, but happy for George and his team.

I'm not just saying these words because they sound like the right things to say. They are heartfelt and sincere. To me it was the epitome of how the game should be played–played for all the right reasons. I think our teams carried that sportsmanship mentality with them even after the seasons had come and gone. They learned a valuable lesson about sports. You can play your heart out, and when all is said and done, you can still congratulate and respect your opponent for his effort. Win or lose, you show the respect for your sport and the respect for your opponent at all times.

I'd like to brag a bit on my school, William Penn High School in New Castle, Delaware. Since the inception of the "State of Delaware Sportsmanship State Championship," our school has won outright or shared the Sportsmanship Trophy every single year. Even a National Sportsmanship Award sits in our trophy case. It's the thing that separates the true winners from the losers. With this approach it is always a win-win situation.

WORKING WITH THE MEDIA

Though coaches might not always count members of the press among the "acres of diamonds" in their landscape, the media will always play an important role in the big game. Whether you like it or not, you must prepare your players for the media coverage that leads up to the game. I was fortunate in my career to have worked with some outstanding sports writers. Matt Zabitka, Kevin Tresolini, Jack Ireland, Buddy Hurlock, and our own local Harold Hoagland are a few that I was privileged to work with and get to know. They were fair to my players and to me. However, it is their job to "hype" the game, and you have to be prepared to deal with the inevitable media pressure in a way that is in your team's best interest.

Players, fans and parents are always interested in what the prediction will be for the game. There is nothing inherently wrong with this, unless your players believe what they read. When your team is the underdog in the contest, you don't want the newspapers to confirm it for them. Too often it seems that teams play to the expectations. Your job is to get your players to rise above the expectations and to play with unprecedented zeal and passion.

The sportswriters are only doing their job, but it is your job to make their pre-game predictions work for your team, not against them. If they pick you to lose, you've got to sell your team on the idea that what others think does not matter. If they pick you to win, you have to convince your team that the game will be won on the field, not in the papers. Ultimately the only thing that matters is what the players believe. If they believe in themselves, in each other, and in you and your staff, that really is all that matters. It becomes an "us against them" mentality. It is a thrilling prospect to do what no one else believes you can do. It grabs the attention and the imagination of the young men and I must admit, even the grizzled veterans of the game. There is no greater thrill in sports than accomplishing the seemingly impossible.

Many coaches shun media coverage. They live in fear of what may or may not be reported. I never believed in that way of thinking. My philosophy was always to see the media as a vehicle to enhance our program. A coach can truly affect his team by what he chooses to say to the media. I have made a list of ten rules to follow while talking with the media. If you adhere to this top-ten guide you'll be on the right track.

My Top Ten Guide to Working with the Media

1. Always talk team success, not individual success.
2. Make no excuses.
3. Congratulate your opponent – win or lose.
4. Thank those who support your program– administration, Boosters, and fans.
5. Talk about hustle, desire, hard work, sacrifice, need for improvement, and sustained focus. (This is reinforcement for your own team.)

6. Talk about one game at a time. (The time to talk about next week is next week.)

7. Share your team goals – not in terms of wins and losses, but in terms of sportsmanship, brotherhood, and building character by doing things the right way.

8. Talk of tradition (the desire to maintain it, add to it, or build it). This brings pride to alumni and former players.

9. Always refer to your players as student-athletes. Make sure your players see that the word "student" comes first. Never lose perspective or forget your main mission – academic and personal improvement through athletic participation.

10. Ask yourself, "Will my comments reflect our core philosophies of team first, never quit attitude, impassioned play, and great sportsmanship?"

That's my top-ten guide to working with the media. If you follow these suggestions, you will never fear the media again. You will embrace them as a partner in promoting your sport as well as your program goals and values.

SCOUTING AND PREPARATION:
Out-thinking Your Opponents

A key principle to success is preparation. Henry Ford said, "Before everything else, getting ready is the secret to success." Preparation starts with doing your homework – scouting. While teaching a military history class, I came across the famous Chinese military strategist and general, Sun Tzu. Sun Tzu wrote the still relevant book *The Art of War*, circa 512 B.C. He didn't coach football, but he could have. His military strategy philosophies are certainly applicable. The one that caught my attention was this famous saying: "So it is said that if you know your enemies and know yourself, you will win a hundred times in a hundred battles. If you only know yourself, but not your opponent, you win one and lose the next. If you do not know yourself or your enemy, you will always lose."

Sun Tzu applied this philosophy to war. Every businessperson, whether he or she knows it or not, has made use of his strategies. A good example is Peter Siris, a Wall Street analyst who wrote a book entitled *Guerilla Investing*. The subtitle to the book is "Winning Strategies for Beating the Wall Street Professionals." He freely quotes from Sun Tzu to outline his strategies to upset the market pros. The titles to his chapters show the Sun Tzu influence. "Know Your Enemy," "Know Yourself," "Avoid the Enemy's Strengths," and "Attack the Enemy's Weaknesses" are illustrations.

I applied Sun Tzu's principles to football: In addition to scouting our opponents, we also had to scout ourselves. In a competitive league your team will not be the only team to scout their opponents. Every game we played had all of our upcoming opponents' scouts in attendance. What are they seeing? You'd better know. What tendencies do you have? Do you call certain plays more often than others? Do you favor the run over the pass or vice versa? Do you have strong first and third down tendencies? Do you have field position tendencies? If you know exactly what your opponents' scouts are seeing from your team, you can better predict what they will do to try to stop you.

It was always a chess match. I liked to be as unpredictable as I could in play calling. The teams that scouted us best probably knew what we were going to do, but didn't know when. It was often better to pass on first down or second down and short, and run on third and long. Quick kicks on third down and long were a staple over the years for us. Fake PATs and punts were practiced every week and used many times during a season. The unpredictability of our calls kept many teams from loading up on us in certain key situations. It also kept them back on their heels and uncertain of what to expect. What made it fun was the fact that our opponents were doing the same thing to us. As I said, it was always a chess match. It can never be a free-lance, "hodgepodge" approach. Your "unpredictability" has to be planned and practiced.

We usually scouted as a group, or in small groups of coaches. However, it is important to assign one top scout to a particular team. Let that assistant take the responsibility for preparing the information on that team personally. With personal responsibility comes motivation and commitment. Of course, the head coach must be involved in scouting the opponents. His most important role, however, is as the final coordinator of all gathered information.

Each position coach should be assigned to scout or to break down film according to his "need to know." Past films and reports should be analyzed and incorporated into the database of current film and game observations. Tendencies will almost always present themselves to you when you do this. The pre-knowledge of what an opponent likes to do in short yardage or long yardage situations, with particular down, distance and location, is invaluable in preparing your offensive and defensive strategies. Determine what types of defensive alignments and adjustments you will see based on the offensive formations you plan to run. You must know your opponent's schemes and adjustments to adequately plan your attack. Obviously, you must also know exactly how you will adjust your own defense to meet the challenges of their offense. Place an equal emphasis on your opponent's kicking game and personnel information. Too many games are lost because of poor kicking game information. Conversely, many of the greatest upsets have come because of great special teams planning.

Knowing the opposing team's personnel strengths and weaknesses is also crucial – especially for play calling. I always wanted to know who our opponent's key players were. Key player information should include the strongest and weakest players equally. Most of my game planning revolved around how to attack the other team's weakest links and how to distract, delay, or avoid their strongest players. When we encountered a particular player who was strong against the run, we ran away from him. If he were quick to pursue, we either countered or ran directly at him. If he liked to penetrate deep, we trapped him. This type of personnel information is invaluable.

Finally, this information must be shared with your team. I liked to "core" the scouting information. "Core" is my acronym for "**c**ategorize" (break it down), "**o**rganize" (put it into teachable form), "**r**epeat" (go over the report multiple times), and "**e**nergize" (get your team excited about how this information will give them the edge). I like the word "core" because good scouting will be truly at the core of your team's success.

Additionally, we followed Eric Butterworth's philosophy when we presented our scouting information to our team. He said, "I tell you and you forget. I show you and you remember. I involve you and you understand." At the beginning of the week we verbally went over the scouting report. Then, we walked our players through the report on the field. The rest of the week we physically ran the plays at them over and over again. By game day, our players knew what to expect. Just to be sure, however, we walked and then ran through the report in the gym the day of the game.

I think it is also important to let your players know how many hours you and your staff have put into this preparation. I was blessed with having outstanding assistant coaches. Each one had individual strengths and abilities that complemented each other. Assistant coach Howdy Duncan was a math teacher and computer buff. He had our scouting material on a computerized program way back in the early 1980s. He gave me a complete tendency chart on plays, down and distance, and field position. Not too many high schools were doing that back then, and I felt it gave us a great advantage. When Howdy retired, Coach Bill Legge joined our staff. Bill had been a former head coach himself and brought a tremendous amount of talent to our program. His ultimate strength, in my opinion, was his scouting ability. He was an absolute master at scouting an opponent. He ran our demo squads in practice against our first team units. With each assistant personally assigned to scout a specific team, and with Coach Legge organizing and running the demo teams, I knew we would always be well prepared.

It is amazing how the players will grow in confidence when they see what you and your staff have done. Remember, when you make that fourth-and-one play call, they must believe in you and in the call. The more you share with them the preparation time that you and your staff have spent, the more likely they will be to trust and believe in the call. More accurately, they must first believe in you! The trust in the call will naturally follow when they believe in you and your staff. To paraphrase Coach Mike Krzyzewski of Duke University: your players must believe in their leader first; then they will buy into your program.

Planning ahead is crucial. Don't wait until the week before the game to prepare. You already know who your biggest rival is, or who will be your best opponent next year. For my team it was usually local powerhouses Newark and Salesianum. In any given year, the state tournament was often decided with a showdown between us and one or both of these teams. So why wait? Don't! Start in the off-season preparing the raw data for the big game. You may need to do certain things differently than you have done them before. If you need to run certain plays or certain formations, you'd better introduce them from day one. You don't want them to be new the week of the game. You don't have to run or show all of them during the season prior to the big game, but you do have to allocate some practice time to them each week if you want to be successful on game day.

Video cut-ups of successful plays against this opponent will reinforce the idea of your team's success against that opponent. Make sure you include positive outcome plays from all aspects of the game (offense, defense, special teams). When you can, include a negative play sequence followed by a positive play. For example, if you can show where your team was penalized but scored or stopped their opponents anyway, show it. If there was a "bad call" in which your team was penalized, but responded with a good play, show it too! You are reinforcing to your team that they will win no matter what happens in the game. Your players are looking for a sign that tells them they can win. Give them the sign ahead of time.

Through great scouting you can prepare your team for any and all eventualities. Do not overlook the sometimes-neglected aspects of the game. When preparing against a particular team, make sure that you go over every possibility that could present itself in the course of the game. On-side kicks, on-side kick returns, how to take a safety, quick kicks, fake kicks, fake kick coverage, fourth-and-one play call, and overtime are a few of the often neglected but important aspects that must be prepared and rehearsed each week.

Great scouting and preparation give you the ability to prepare your team for all circumstances. Take the time to develop these most important components to create the chance to pull off the upset.

WEIGHTS AND CONDITIONING

Even the best scouting and preparation can't make up for players that are not physically ready to play their best. Instead of lamenting that your players are not "bigger, faster and stronger," take the initiative and make them bigger, faster, and stronger!

If you do not have a weight room, create your own. We started our weight room in a storage closet in the wrestling room. I personally ran the summer weight room three days a week from 8:00 A.M. to 10:00 A.M., 12:00 noon to 2:00 P.M., and 6:00 P.M. to 8:00 P.M. in the initial years of our program. I did not want the time of day to be an excuse for anyone. If a player worked a summer job at night, he came at 8:00 A.M. or noon. If he had summer school, he came at noon or 6:00 P.M. — no excuses, just commitment.

I studied the weightlifting programs of Bill Starr and the Philadelphia Eagles' longtime trainer Otho Davis (Duke football trainer during my playing days). I wrote my own weightlifting manual and workbook based on their programs. This formed the base for the early gains that our team made in the area of strength and conditioning. I also got help from a former teammate of mine at William

Penn, Richard Hayford. Captain (now Colonel) Hayford was teaching physical education at West Point and was an invaluable source of information for our weightlifting program. My good friend and weightlifting Coach Neale Clopper and I spent some quality time with Richard at West Point.

Later, we also brought in legendary motivator and weightlifting guru Dr. Greg Shepard, founder of "Bigger, Faster, Stronger." We felt that we had to take our weights and conditioning program to the next level and that Dr. Shepard and his program were the answer. We were right! He personally flew in to be with us and put on a fantastic weightlifting and motivational clinic in 1986. We made our kids "Bigger, Faster, Stronger" thanks to hard work and a lot of help from Dr. Greg Shepard. To this day, the principles of Dr. Shepard's program are still the foundation of the William Penn program.

If I had to start a program tomorrow, the first thing I would do is call Dr. Shepard. I would raise the money to bring him or one of his great associates in to put on their "Be An 11" clinic. The "11" concept has at its roots the developing of "a person who holds himself or herself to the highest possible standards in order to attain his or her highest possible destiny." For me, that is what coaching is all about–the development of the total person. I would purchase his *Be An 11 Guidebook for Success* for each person on my staff and one for each player. The BFS *Bigger, Faster, Stronger* motivational magazine is also a must.

Each year we purchased the BFS weightlifting workbook and taught every player how to use it to record his workout. Dr. Shepard always said that you have to measure and record each workout in order to achieve your goals. We took that to heart. The daily records were used as a measure for us to work diligently against in order to break our personal bests. His system of "Dot Drills" for quickness and plyometrics for explosive strength were also great complementary programs. Because of the "Bigger, Faster, Stronger" program, our strength levels and our confidence were second to none.

URGENCY — "NOW" PRACTICE

With scouting, planning, and fitness programs in place, your practice sessions have the potential for maximum effectiveness. To achieve that maximum, you and your team must always have a sense of urgency. If you only go through the motions in practice, you will accomplish very little. Long protracted practice sessions usually undermine the sense of urgency. Break down your practice sessions into small intense segments. Each segment must have a specific focus and goal. Your sessions must be centered on the basic fundamentals. Josh Waitzkin, a grandmaster chess player, says, "It is rarely a mysterious technique that drives us to the top, but rather a profound mastery of what may well be a basic skill set." This philosophy has direct application to football and winning.

Let's face it; if your team can't block, tackle, run, catch and throw at a high proficiency level, your chances for success will be slim to none. You must make your players see that what they are doing in practice right now has direct application to the upcoming game and season.

Another factor affected by this "now" approach is timing. Think about it: if you practice without the sense of urgency, your game timing will be off. Game day brings an automatic sense of urgency complete with increased adrenalin. Your players in game situations will play faster with more hype. If you do not try to simulate this tempo of movement in practice, the timing and mesh of your plays will be jeopardized. Teams who do not practice with the sense of urgency are usually the ones who fumble snaps, miss hand-offs, and under- or over-throw their targets. We felt that our intense "now" oriented practices conditioned our players to react and play with the desired and heightened sense of urgency. Correspondingly this allowed them to play and react quickly in the real games.

We also wanted them to think "now" on each and every play of the game. Games are often won or lost on a handful of plays. How many times have you seen two teams slug it out, only to have one play separate the victor from the loser? One run, pass, fumble, interception, missed assignment, penalty or blocked kick will often be the margin of victory. Our point to our team was, how do you know which play will be the one? When you line up for the next play, you just don't know whether or not this will be the game-breaking play. Since you can never know when, you should play each down as if it were "the one."

You have to prepare your team to see each and every down as the opportunity to make the difference. A team that can master that relentless mindset will be a force to be reckoned with. Your mantra should be, "This is the play, right here and right now! This one will be the one!" Make your players "now" conscious and then watch the sense of urgency start to infuse their mindset, and consequently, their efforts and the results.

KEY FUNDAMENTALS

There are certain key football fundamentals that must be part of your daily preparation for the upset. I've made a list of my top ten. There are many more than ten key fundamentals, but I am focusing here on my pick for the top ten only. If you make these ten fundamentals your coaching priority, you will have established a solid base that will mold your team into a contender—anywhere, anytime.

1. The Snap

The first and most important offensive fundamental is the snap – the center-to-quarterback exchange. No offensive play can start without the snap. It is a component of 100% of your plays from scrimmage. What else can compare? This often-overlooked fundamental must be worked on and drilled daily.

The snap was the single most important factor in the 1996 championship game with our perennial rival, Newark High School (coached by their longtime excellent coach, Butch Simpson). The game was played in the worst field conditions that I have ever encountered in my entire playing and coaching career. We played in a driving rainstorm on a field that was as slippery as an ice skating rink. That great day was made most memorable by the fact that we did not have one bad snap all day long. That statistic includes having not one bad long snap in the kicking game, as well. Only those who witnessed that game can fully appreciate that statistic. It truly was the difference in the game.

There are many ways to give and receive the snap. Taught and drilled properly, they can all be effective. The most important coaching point, however, does not involve the method of snap, but the patience required by the center and quarterback during the execution of the snap. That is the single most important ingredient. Most snap fumbles occur because either the center or the quarterback rushes the snap process. Centers get anxious to get out and block their opponent while quarterbacks want to get out of there and execute the run or pass. This occurs usually at the most critical times in the game, often on third or fourth downs and in the red zones at either end of the field.

The center and the quarterback are especially vulnerable to this mistake the closer to the goal line they get. Teach the center to finish the snap and the follow-through motions completely before anything else is attempted. The quarterback has to be patient enough to ride the hands forward as the center steps and to have the ball firmly under control before moving out from under center. Make this an automatic procedure through repetitive drills and constant coaching reminders. It will pay huge dividends when the pressure is on and you need to make the big play.

2. Fumble Prevention and Recovery

The second most important fundamental is actually a combination of two things: fumble prevention and fumble recovery.

Fumbling the football is one of the most critical errors that a team can make. It not only stops a drive, but it is also a tremendous momentum shifter. We practiced our anti-fumble drills every day from the first day of practice to the last.

We put our backs and ends through the "Slap Alley" drill. In order to do this drill successfully without fumbling, the runner first must be instructed on how to hold the ball. The fingertips should cover the front tip of the ball, with one side of the ball pressed against the ribs and the other side covered by the bicep. We constantly checked this ball position by pounding on the ball from on top and from the bottom. It should never come loose if held this way. When the player is running, the ball simply slides up and down on the ribs and never loses contact with the ribs. The rest of the "Slap Alley" drill consists of a runner and two lines of defenders. The runner, from only one yard away, dips and explodes into the two defenders located directly in front of him while delivering a shoulder blow. (You can vary the start of this drill with a hand-off if you choose.) After the two defenders finish delivering their initial blow, they let the runner go to the next players in line. Their job is not to deliver a blow, but to try to strip the ball from the runner. If the runner has his head down and is not running in balance, they simply push him down. Too many runners lean too far forward when in traffic and go down too easily. The runner, using short choppy steps, then goes through the rest of the line. When the last defenders in line have had their try at stripping the ball, the runner breaks out and makes a cut on a final defender or coach stationed approximately five yards from the last two players in the "Slap Alley" line. After the player makes the cut, he sprints the last ten yards for a score. A coach is watching the whole drill. If the runner cuts too soon or too late on the last defender, he learns the error of his ways. If the runner fumbles the ball, he must recover his own fumble and then return to start the drill all over again. We have found this drill to be the number one drill to prevent fumbles.

One final note on fumble prevention must be made. We never let our players catch a ball without "looking the ball" into the hands (exaggerate this) and then securing the ball properly while running an extra ten yards after the catch. Too many players practice catching the ball and never finish it off by putting the ball away. Laziness in practice will come back to haunt them. Require your players always to finish off the catch, and it will become instinctive and automatic.

To help your receivers, you can modify the "Slap Alley" drill for them. Throw them a short pass and then have them look the ball into their hands, secure the football, and then run after the catch through the "Slap Alley" drill. Soon, the transitions of catch, secure, and run will be smooth and automatic. Your team will also enjoy watching the turnover ratio steadily improve in your favor.

Recovering a fumble is a skill that must also be taught and practiced. Too many players (particularly in the NFL) do not do it properly. Too often they try to pick up the ball in traffic and end up either booting it or not recovering it at all. We taught from day one that a fumble must be recovered on the ground. The player must get down beside the ball and use his arms to draw it in to the stomach. The body must then curl into a fetal position and protect the ball completely. The player should resemble an armadillo, with nothing but knees, elbows, and pads exposed.

The only time we wanted our players to scoop up a loose football and run was when the player definitely knew that he was all alone, or his teammates yelled for him to pick it up. We practiced this "scoop" technique (like a shortstop, with knees bent, hands under the ball, scooping it towards his own goal line) as well. If however, he were not absolutely sure, he was to get on the ground and cover the ball. Our defensive ends actually practiced the "scoop" drill every day, all year long.

We practiced the fumble recovery drill with the entire team every day in pre-season. We incorporated it into our two-man sled drills. We had two players deliver three blows to the two-man sled. Starting in a three-point stance, they would hit and recover three times. After the third hit, they would seat-roll out, scramble up, and look for the fumbled football. The coach would throw the ball out and then demand that the proper fumble recovery technique be used.

3. Ball Handling

Third on my fundamental must list is ball handling. Poor ball handling will lead to fumbles. We did ball handling drills every day of the year. Our favorite one was a simple but effective drill. The players are divided into two lines. The first player in line has the ball tucked away while running toward the first player in the opposite line. The runner with the ball always holds the ball with two hands as he moves it into position for the hand-off to the other player. As they pass each other, the ball handler puts the ball out at hip level and looks it into the pocket of the receiver. The receiver holds his inside arm up and parallel to the ground, out of the way. His opposite hand is placed on his hip and acts as a stopper for the ball. This "stopper" hand prevents the ball from being placed beyond the pocket. The receiver dips over the ball as he takes the hand-off and immediately secures the ball properly. A coach should be positioned at the hand-off spot to watch and critique the drill. Since we used a double hand-off play, this drill was invaluable for our backs (not just the quarterbacks).

4. Quarterback Throws—or Not?

Fourth on the list is teaching the quarterback when to throw and, sometimes more importantly, when not to throw. Too many quarterbacks wait for the receiver to get open before they throw the ball. That's why we always told our quarterbacks in practice to throw "now!" Most practice sessions with quarterbacks and receivers reveal the fatal flaw of waiting for the receiver to get open before the ball is thrown. That just doesn't work in real games. In every pass route there comes a point when the "cut" will be made to get open. The quarterback has to anticipate the receiver's "cut" and throw immediately. If he waits, he allows the defender to recover and move to the ball with the receiver.

In his study of martial arts, Josh Waitzkin discovered a nineteenth century Chinese philosopher named Wu Yu-Hsiang, who said, "At the opponent's slightest move, I move first." Only through repetitive "throw now" practice will the quarterback learn to throw to the spot where the receiver will be after the cut. Timing is always critical in the passing game, and there really is no shortcut to develop it.

Even more critical is for the quarterback to understand the importance of learning when not to throw. Too many quarterbacks try to "gun" the ball into covered receivers. The quarterback has to be trained to know the down and distance and then act and throw accordingly. There is most definitely a time to "eat" the ball and a time to throw it away. Some players can throw off their back foot while falling away, but that is the exception. We tried to train our quarterbacks to throw while balanced. Footwork drills are important to simulate throwing after the required steps in a drop are completed. Throwing on the run in both directions must be practiced daily. Scrambling drills with pressure should also be a part of the daily practice routine.

We did not have too many hard and fast rules as to what not to do, but there are a few that should be taught. The first "do not" rule: Do not throw across your body (you're going one way and you try to throw back the other way by throwing across your body) to the middle or opposite side of the field. When you do this, velocity and accuracy are severely reduced and you are inviting an interception.

The second rule: Never throw while off balance. This rule is similar to the first rule. Off balance throws are usually weak and inaccurate. There are exceptions, however. On short passes and screen passes, the quarterback has to find the open alley to complete the throw. Sometimes the only way to get the ball to the receiver is by throwing an awkward and off balance throw. With practice, you can get away with this on the short passes only. If the quarterback must throw off balance on a longer throw, I would rather have him tuck the ball and get what he can get running. Even a sack is better than an interception.

The third rule: Never under-throw (unless it is done intentionally) or throw with too flat a trajectory when going deep. The ball should be arced high and long. Our mantra on the deep pass was always, "He gets it or no one gets it."

The fourth rule: Never throw the ball up and inside on a sideline or out pattern. Always throw down and away on these patterns. The receiver should come back to the ball and lose some ground on the break. We never wanted a pass thrown up and in where a defender could recover and intercept. The long sideline pass is probably the most difficult and dangerous pass to make for a high school quarterback. An interception there is usually six points for the other team.

The fifth rule: Never throw where you haven't looked. This is especially critical on screen passes. It's great to look off defenders, but never begin a throw before looking. I have seen too many passes picked off by a defender who was standing right in the line of fire. Receivers get bumped off course, they get knocked down, they slip, and coverages change. One look at the receiver and the interception would have been avoided.

There are obviously many more coaching points in the passing game, but these are the ones that we concentrated on. Concentrating on these five rules will dramatically cut down on your interception rate.

5. Catching the Ball

The fifth fundamental is catching the ball. It might seem obvious; everyone today practices throwing and catching. It is a huge part of modern-day football. However, too many coaches do not drill the components of the catch. One of the best things that I did early in my career was to get the pass catching drills made famous by the Baltimore Colts Hall of Fame receiver Raymond Berry. Raymond Berry's net receiving drills are fantastic. The receiver must catch the ball low to each side, mid-height and high to each side. The ball is then thrown directly at the receiver, low, mid and high. The receiver turns and catches the ball over each shoulder and must veer to catch the ball.

One-hand catches (to improve hand strength), staying in bounds catches, and diving catches are also incorporated. The quarterback or coach is only ten yards away, and the receiver stands in front of a large net. The net allows for many throws with little time needed for the retrieval of footballs. This drill provides the receivers with ten times the number of catches that they would receive in a normal practice session.

The other critical catch is the catch of a punt. This one catching skill has probably cost more teams games than any other. Without a good skilled punt returner, you are doomed to lost yards and to muffs recovered by the other team. Most punts that are not caught will bounce for another 10, 15, or 20 yards. That's lost yards to you and that means poor field position. A muffed punt is usually a turnover. Most turnovers usually mean a momentum shift and more often than not, points for the other team.

My former coach, Bill Cole, was an outstanding collegiate punt returner at the University of Delaware. He took this skill to heart and developed a terrific coaching program for our punt returners. He taught our players how to read the spin of the ball, judge the wind, play a bounce, and make the sure catch. Through scouting, he knew exactly how deep they should be to receive the kick, and they learned when and where to make (or not make) the catch. His priority was always the catch, first and foremost. The return after the catch was always a bonus for us, but even that was worked on daily. Too many coaches neglect this skill; Bill had our players working on it before, during and after practice each day. It paid off!

6. Blocking

The sixth fundamental that must be mastered is blocking. Good blocking is, of course, essential to the success of your team. You can't run, throw, or kick without good blocking. There are too many good drills that you can employ to list them; however, seven-man sleds are good for firing off as a team and maintaining good position and leg drive. Two-man sleds are even better because they require a player to stay with the sled and maintain a good blocking surface and posture. Nothing, however, beats live one-on-one or two-on-one blocking drills. No sled or dummy ever made can simulate the movement of a real live defender. Pick your drills and do them daily. Quarterback sacks, blocked kicks, or punts and negative rushing yardage are killers. Move this up to your number one priority if you prefer – it will pay off!

7. Tackling

Number seven on the list (but number one on any defensive fundamental list) is tackling. How many games have been lost because of poor tackling? Too many! Form tackling drills should be done every day. We used a set routine. We did one step right shoulder, one step left shoulder, running right shoulder, running left shoulder, straight ahead no fake by runner, and straight ahead one fake allowed by the runner tackling drills. Our coaching points were always "Keep your head up, slide it to the side (never spear or lead with the head), and then shoulder neck squeeze." This was accomplished to the cadence of "dip, hit, wrap, and drive." If you make these drills a priority, you will see vast improvement over time in your team's tackling performance.

8. Angles of Pursuit

Number eight is angles of pursuit. Too many players run to where the ball is, instead of where it is going to be. We worked daily on our angles of pursuit. When your team pursues properly, you will drastically cut down on the number of long runs and long touchdowns. We liked to have our pursuit angles form a "picket fence" that had to be crossed whenever the ball was run against us. We always wanted to string any run out to our "twelfth man," the sideline. The sideline has never missed a tackle in the history of the game! If a runner chose to cut back we wanted to be in position to intercept him and prevent the long run.

The most important rule in pursuit angle is that a player should never follow directly behind another teammate. Take and fill a different lane to the ball carrier. The second rule is never to overrun the ball carrier. When you take the improper angle and overrun the carrier, you allow him to cut back behind you. The final rule is simple: hustle!

If you've been counting, that is eight of my top ten key fundamentals. I listed six offensive and two defensive fundamentals (these eight apply to the kicking game as well). As I mentioned earlier, there are hundreds of key fundamentals to this game, but I wanted to stay within the framework of a top ten list. In order to add the last two to complete the list of ten, I'm going to leave out many important ones. However, I think these last two non-physical fundamentals are critical to any list. The last two I would categorize under the heading "Mental Key Fundamentals."

9. Know Your Assignments

Number nine on the list is "Know your assignments." There can be no "C" players on a football team. Everyone must be an "A" student on the field. Everyone must know his position thoroughly. Every blocking assignment, every route, and every coverage must be automatic. Not knowing an assignment on a play causes busted plays, sacks, interceptions, and illegal procedure calls. All of these are game killers. Our coaches (especially our line coaches) quizzed their players on their assignments regularly. In pre-season the quizzing was done daily. Poor grades were rewarded with sprint work at the end of practice. Lack of assignment knowledge usually resulted in lack of confidence, and therefore, lack of aggressive play. Not only was the wrong guy blocked but also the wrong guy was blocked non-aggressively. The extra confusion also resulted in offside penalties, illegal procedure calls, and forgotten snap counts. None of this is positive. Most of it can be minimized and eliminated by insisting that all players learn their plays.

10. Clock Management

The tenth and last key fundamental is for the coach. It is time or clock management. I don't know how many games I have seen (at all levels) that have been lost because of poor time management. Conversely, good time management has won many games. Study the rules and know what starts and stops the clock. Practice how to run and how to slow down the clock. Teach your players the basic rules of staying in bounds when you're trying to run out the clock and getting out of bounds when you need it to stop. Teach them how to hurry up and get set so a play can be run or the ball spiked to stop the clock. Create time, down, field position, and score situations for your team to practice. For example, tell them that the score is 14-12 in favor of their opponent. There are only two minutes remaining in the fourth quarter, and they are on their own 35-yard line with first down and ten to go and one time-out left. They will soon get the feel for the special "two-minute" drill. With enough practice, they will have the confidence to run it in a real game and be calm and poised while doing so. Clock management is essential to score that winning touchdown or field goal.

MORE ON DEFENSE

You might have noticed that my "top ten" list of key fundamentals includes only two defensive keys. I stand by my list, but I have to say that defense was, and rightfully so, truly our top priority. I wanted hard-nosed defense to define our program because defense is not just a system or a skill—it is an attitude. That attitude affects all aspects of the game. After all, we wanted to win, and nothing affects the outcome of a game more than defense. Why? It's simple: if the other team can't score, we can't lose. The worst-case score scenario will be 0-0. But that will not usually be the case. Don't forget that the defense can score too. A great play by defense will give your offense the ball back many times and in good field position. Without great defense, there will be no upset.

As I have previously mentioned, defensively, more tight games are lost by poor tackling play than probably any other reason. Tackling fundamentals must be reinforced and drilled each day of the season. They form the core of your defensive success. Our team constantly worked on proper tackling technique, pursuit angles, and hustle. We worked on this every day of the year right up to the last practice before the final championship game. Tackling technique is a skill; taking proper pursuit angles is a matter of great team discipline. Combine the two and you have a powerful defense.

The final piece of the puzzle is for you to put the people on the field that will hustle and never quit until the whistle blows. Pursuit angle drills emphasize the attitude of the defense. Less talented individuals can combine to become a great defense. You can teach tackling and demand great hustle. Don't play talented kids who won't hustle. You will find out who wants to play when you work on your pursuit angles. That defensive end opposite the ball will take off on a deep angle of pursuit only if he is disciplined and committed to doing so. Chasing after a fleet ball carrier across the entire field might go unrewarded ninety-nine out of a hundred times. That one time, however, when the ball carrier cuts back and you are there to meet him, makes it all worthwhile. That one time may be the difference in the outcome of the game. Remember what I stated earlier: if they can't score, you can't lose.

The great Civil War general William Tecumseh Sherman summed up our philosophy of defense. He said, "Get there the fastest with the mostest!" We used the acronym "HAM" to describe this style of play. "HAM" stood for "Hostile, Agile, and Mobile." We added one thing to this, however; we wanted our players there fast, but only after they had completed all of their reads and techniques. Then and only then did they break full throttle to the ball. One of the worst things you can do is to allow your team to go out of control to chase the ball.

A good team will counter, reverse, and screen you to death. Our backside defenders always stayed home and read for counter, reverse, or screen. When the ball going away from them crossed the line of scrimmage, then and only then would they break on their deep pursuit angles. We wanted to create a picket fence with our pursuit. If a ball carrier tried to cut back across the field, he had to cross our fence line of defenders.

As I outlined in my top ten key fundamentals (number eight), our rules were simple. When you are taking a proper pursuit angle, never follow in the same line of pursuit as your teammate; create some space between. We wanted to take a deeper angle than he was taking. We never wanted two defenders occupying the same space. When the spacing is too close, one blocker can take both defenders out with one block. Spacing creates levels of pursuit and builds the picket fence that we always wanted to have in place. If your players are disciplined in their approach, they can then turn on the burners to get to the ball carrier.

Another rule already mentioned was never to over-run the ball carrier. When we were closing in on the runner, we wanted to gauge our speed to his. We wanted to be under control and converge on the runner on an angle that moved him toward the sideline whenever possible. We also wanted to make the sure tackle, not the diving tackle. The diving tackle was always a last-ditch effort for us to prevent a touchdown. If we were alone on the tackle, we taught our players to wrap high on the player. Even if it meant that he carried us a few extra yards, that was all right. Again, we wanted to ensure that the tackle was made. Our other pursuers should be there shortly to finish off the tackle if need be.

Very few runners ever cut back against the grain for long runs against us. When it did occur, it was either an obvious mistake by someone taking an improper angle of pursuit or a lack of hustle. Lack of hustle, however, should never occur and should never be tolerated. Part of the hustle to the ball included what we called "swarm." "Swarm" for us meant everyone moves to the ball on a full sprint after their responsibilities have been completed. We broke down around the ball carrier and helped to finish off the tackle. Those who arrived last to the ball were to stay just outside the "swarm" of tacklers and take a "break down" position between the ball carrier and the goal.

For me this was important. How many times have you seen a horde of tacklers all over the ball carrier, only to have him break out of the pile and score? It happens too often. Our way of preventing this was to have the total team "swarm" and surround the ball. The last ones there would act as super safeties to prevent the break-out run. I don't recall any pile break-outs after we instituted our version of the "swarm."

The final component was the "hustle." Hustling is one area where your team can be the best in the world! That's right; your team can be number one and second to none in the critical area of hustle. Hustle is a mental and physical condition that any player can possess and demonstrate at the highest level, regardless of skill or athleticism. It is your job as the coach to demand hustle and teach it to your team.

One way to achieve hustle is to demand that your team never look tired. This becomes a psychological factor for your opponent as well. When it is the fourth quarter and they are getting tired, let them see your team still sprinting. On offense we demanded that our center break our huddle first, followed by the rest of the team. Our quarterback would call the play and then send the center up to the ball in a full ten-yard sprint. He did this on the first play of the game right up to the very last. The quarterback repeated the play for the rest of the team and then "broke" them into a full sprint up to the ball. When you're tired and you see the other team doing this every play, it wears on you. It gives them an aura of invincibility.

Many teams have been "psyched out" by this tireless display of hustle. It also has a game advantage factor built into it as well. Simply put, we usually ran more plays than our opponents. Because we got out of the huddle so quickly, we saved valuable clock time. Those extra plays start to add up and become a great advantage by the end of the game. If any player did not hustle out of the huddle and up to the ball, he was replaced. In practice, our quarterback was instructed to bring back to the huddle any group that did not break the huddle properly and sprint to the ball. If the quarterback did not bring them back, one of our coaches did. Often we had an assistant coach watch exclusively for this.

We even took it a little farther. On defense, the linebacker who called the defensive signals had the authority to send to the sideline any player who did not break our huddle our way. We gave our quarterback on offense the same authority. One of our first great linebackers was a team captain by the name of Frank Kaminski. He took this duty to heart and more than once during practice and in games expelled one of his teammates from the huddle. He simply told the offending player to go to the sideline and see the coach. They knew he had the authority and obeyed.

One of my favorite stories regarding Frank actually came after he graduated and went to Ferrum to play collegiate ball for Hank Norton. At a clinic in Washington D.C., I met up with some of the Ferrum coaches. They told me that in one of their games Frank banished one of his teammates to the sideline—just as he had done in high school. The player came running off the field to the dismay of the defensive coaches. They yelled at him, "Why are you coming out?" He replied that Frank had told him to leave! What a leader! The Ferrum coaches were not initially pleased with Frank's on-field coaching, but when he explained to them that that was how it was done at his high school and the reason why, they changed their opinion. I don't think they continued to let Frank do this, but I do know that they had a newfound respect for Frank's leadership and his demand for "hustle."

For me, hustle is a by-product of passion. Passion for the game is a must. I wanted every coach and every player to approach everything we did with passion. One of the best ways to define passion can be found in John C. Maxwell's book *The 21 Indispensable Qualities of a Leader*. Maxwell relates a conversation between the philosopher Socrates and a young man:

It is said that a dispassionate young man approached the Greek philosopher Socrates and casually stated, "O great Socrates, I come to you for knowledge."

The philosopher took the man down to the sea and dunked him under the water for thirty seconds. When he let the young man up for air, Socrates asked him to repeat what he wanted.

"Knowledge, O great one," he sputtered. Socrates put him under the water again, only that time a little longer. After repeated dunkings and responses, the philosopher asked, "What do you want?" The young man finally gasped, "Air, I want air!"

"Good," answered Socrates. "Now, when you want knowledge as much as you wanted air, you shall have it."

The point is simple. If you want to win the big game, or be successful in any pursuit in life, do it with passion!

PLAYING IN BAD WEATHER

Playing in bad weather can offer a great opportunity to overcome obstacles and turn a negative into a positive. For some teams, playing in bad weather is a problem and becomes an obstacle to their success. No one wants to play on wet and rainy days (except linemen). For many coaches and teams, a rainy day is viewed as a negative. The thinking goes like this: the footing will be bad, fumbles will occur, passes will be dropped, it will favor the heavier team, and on and on ad nauseam.

I think we learned how to deal with bad weather the best possible way. We turned it into a plus for our team. When I played for Coach Bill L. Cole in the early to mid-sixties (1962–1966), he told us that we were "mudders." He said that because of our proximity to the Delaware River, there was a correlation between our success and bad weather. He said, "There's something in the water." Of course, he probably said this with tongue in cheek, but as a ninth grade kid I believed in it, and, to tell you the truth, I think he did, too! He told us that for some reason we always played better than the other team in wet or rainy conditions. I adopted that view and preached it to my team when I became the head coach. I simply repeated what I had learned and believed as a young player myself. It is amazing how that thinking can change your view on those cold and rainy days. When others were worrying about playing under the adverse conditions, we were not. Part of my pre-game speech would mention that this was exactly what we wanted. We loved it because we were "mudders" – the advantage was ours.

We also prepared for it. One drill for quarterbacks involved a bucket of water and some rubber balls. Our budget never allowed us to soak our good leather footballs. It's not the ball, anyway, but the idea that you are preparing for poor conditions that matters most. We stressed holding onto the football with more palm exposed to the ball and not just fingertips. We also stressed that the ball was to be held in two hands at all times until the final release of the pass. We stressed this all of the time anyway to diminish fumbles on blind-sided hits.

One thing that I did one year early in my career was go to the local airport weather station and get data on precipitation in our area for the months of September through the first week in December. (With today's computers you can access this information with a "Google" search.) Those dates coincided with our season and the state championship tournament. I found that historically in any given year we would be playing 30 per cent of the time on a wet field or in rain. This knowledge was always passed on to our team. This way they were expecting it. They were forearmed with the knowledge that we would play in wet weather and forearmed with the knowledge that we were "mudders." Put the two together and we knew we could win.

Our best exhibition of this came in the state championship game in 1996 against our archrival, Newark High School. As I mentioned earlier in the book, we played the game in a driving rainstorm that had the field in the worst condition that I have ever experienced in my entire playing and coaching career. Both teams and fans should be commended for braving the elements that day. A person couldn't even walk across the field without slipping and sliding. We won that state championship game. The thing that I am most proud of, however, is that we played the entire game without one quarterback-center exchange fumble–not one! For me that was the ultimate. Anyone who was there that day could tell you that it was almost a miracle under those terrible conditions. For our team, however, it was no miracle–after all, we were "mudders"!

The weather was also a factor in my decision on what type of offense and defense we would run. You have to know where you play. In Delaware the weather is good for most of the season. However, when tournament time rolls around in late November and early December, conditions can be brutal at times. We played one state championship game in winds that were howling between 30 and 40 miles an hour, sending the wind-chill factor down below zero. Because of this, our philosophy was simple. We would make great defense our number one priority. We could concentrate on our kicking game to maximize our field position, and we would be a play action passing team that featured the run first. Don't let this fool you. When we had great passing quarterbacks and receivers, we threw the ball as much as anyone, but that was never our emphasis. We knew that come tournament time, the weather would not allow us to throw as much as we might want to do. But no weather would stop our running game. I really can't recall too many teams that have won championships at the high school, college, and even pro level that did not run the ball well.

Unless you play all of your games in a dome, it would be wise to fashion your style of play to accommodate the type of weather and conditions that you expect to encounter. Three of the seven state championship games that we won were accomplished by throwing no pass longer than 12 to 15 yards–all off play-action. The weather conditions just wouldn't allow more.

This is just another example of taking the negative and making it a positive. Remember, success and the big upsets begin in the mind. Each team is physically affected in the same way by bad weather; therefore, the team that mentally deals with it best and prepares for it best will win the contest. So place the positive seed thoughts in your players' minds and "water" them daily; soon, your team will believe that no weather obstacles exist. Their only thought will be: The worse the weather, the more it "enhances our chances."

THE PEP TALK

P re-game pep talks are important. The pep talk is the final phase of the effort to inspire your players for the big game. They've watched the inspirational movie and listened to the carefully selected motivational music. Parents, coaching staff, and other support groups have provided preparation and encouragement. Now it's your turn to set the final mental and emotional stage right before the kickoff. I loved this time! The waiting is finally over, nerves are on edge, and all of your staff's and team's hard work is about to go on display for all to see. The expectations were always high and exhilarating.

Every coach has tried in his career to give a Knute Rockne pep talk–one that will be inspirational and remembered, a pep talk that will literally have your players roaring out of the locker room. Just make sure you have them going out the correct door. Don't laugh! It didn't happen to me, but I have heard many stories over the years about teams that were all fired up and sent streaking to a closet door or a locked one. A traffic jam and chaos to rival rush hour ensues, followed by a resultant flat tire of enthusiasm! Now, back to the pep talk. Everyone has his own style. Be yourself. Trying to be Rockne or

Vince Lombardi on game day just won't work for everyone. In my opinion, the best pre-game pep talks are short and sweet. I am convinced that the best pre-game talk that I ever gave went something like this: "Our team has worked hard. Our players and coaches are totally prepared. We know exactly what to do and how to do it. To tell you the truth, there isn't another team on the face of the earth that I would rather be with right here and right now than you!"

That was it. I walked out of the locker room. That speech was not the reason that we won the 1991 state championship that day against one of the finest teams that Delaware had ever seen, but I felt it was all that our team needed–short, focused and to the point.

Another pre-game strategy that we used was again nothing earth-shattering. On more than one occasion, our pre-game talk centered on the visualization of our opening play or sequence of plays. I would ask our players to close their eyes. When all eyes were closed, I would then call out our opening offensive play of the game. After repeating the play, I would break the imaginary huddle and call out our cadence. On "Hike!" each player was asked to visualize himself running the play according to his specific assignment. The center had to see himself snap the ball and then fire off into his block. The quarterback had to see himself receive the snap and then make the hand-off and carry out his fake. Every player right down the line was to see the perfect play in his mind. I thought this technique helped us to concentrate and to calm down the mental jitters that often occur on the first series of a game.

As far as half-time talks went, for us that was a time for adjustments and re-focusing. My team broke down into its position components with their respective position coach and went over everything we had experienced in that first half. If blocking adjustments needed to be made, we made them then. I also talked with all of my assistants and spotters and got their input on what plays we needed to run or not run. Half time was preparation and adjustment time, not inspiration time. There were usually only three things that I ever took time to talk about at half time. First, if we were ahead, I cautioned the team about letting down. Now was the time to push even harder. We always said the score was 0-0, regardless of the actual score. Second, if we were behind, I would always remind them that the best teams will find themselves behind at half time in the course of a season at least two or three times. In other words, they should not panic. The best teams know that if they persevere and give their all one play at a time, they will find a way to win. Third, if their effort in the first half had been less than what we demanded, I challenged them and called upon their pride. That was about it—methodical, no panic, and no wholesale changes. Even our adjustments were just that. They were practiced adjustments that were integrated into our players' minds starting from the first day of practice.

Have I ever deviated from the above? Yes I have, and usually with devastating results. Unpracticed changes hardly ever work. They lead to a sense of confusion and aid in the "downward spiral" effect on your team. When things are not going well, a coach who "grab-bags" for a way to win is conveying to his team that they need a miracle. It is much better to stay the course and make minor adjustments based on what your players know and know how to do best. This gives them confidence that if they go out in the second half and execute better the things that they do best, they will eventually win. You can't have confidence in something you have never done before. So coach, that's my pep talk for you! Now, "Go get 'em!" But first, check that you're heading for the right door!

GAME STRATEGY AND PLAY CALLING:
The "Hedgehog" Philosophy

Game day strategy and play calling should not be too elaborate. Go with what got you there. Too many coaches make the mistake of trying to put in too many "new" things for the big game. My father, the Reverend Brooks E. Reynolds, a Methodist minister, was always preaching Steven Covey's theme: "The main thing is to keep the main thing the main thing." You can apply that to any phase of your life. In football it has its own application: concentrate on what you know how to do best. Stay within your system. Stay with your basic philosophy of offense and defense. Go with what you've practiced a thousand times. Players can't have the necessary experience and confidence in wholesale changes before the big game. Stay with the core plays and base defenses that they know. That allows you to "nibble" at the corners with a few well-selected adjustments or "wrinkles." But always remember, ". . . keep the main thing the main thing."

Jim Collins, in his book *Good to Great*, calls this the "Hedgehog Concept." Collins took this idea from Isaiah Berlin's essay "The

Hedgehog and the Fox." The story is based on an ancient Greek parable. The fox is a cunning and gifted hunter. It is clever and devises a multitude of ways to attack and eat the hedgehog, but the hedgehog always wins. Collins says, "The fox knows many things, but the hedgehog knows one big thing." Every time the hedgehog is attacked, he simply rolls himself into a ball and withstands the attack. He does what he knows how to do best. His defense is simple and direct. He knows how to do this instinctively and without hesitation. Collins says that this is what businesses have to do to become great. They have to keep things simple and do what they do best.

Football is no different. To be successful, you need to do the core things well, and you need to do that which you know how to do best. This is especially true when you are in a tight game and things are not going well. Instead of "grab-bagging" for gimmick plays and wildly calling miracle plays to catch up, just stop, regroup, and go back to basics. Go back to your core offensive and defensive plays. Let your players rebuild their confidence on the plays they know the best.

This also works when you find yourself in mid-season and not playing particularly well. Instead of panicking and changing everything as so many coaches do, do the opposite: start small. Take the six core running plays and the six core passing plays and run only those plays. You need to concentrate on perfecting these and only these plays. Depth, not breadth, is your goal. You want your players to become experts on these base plays. Run your base defense and make the team work out the necessary adjustments rather than changing defenses. You don't change horses in midstream, yet this is exactly what I have observed so many young coaches do time and time again. Get simple! Go back and emphasize basic skill drills. Go back to your tackling and blocking drills. Re-teach the fundamentals. Then apply them to your base plays. Your team will soon be acting and reacting and not having to think about what to do. Instead they will be doing it naturally–just like the hedgehog.

The simpler you make your offense, the better the outcome will be for your team. I like to call the basic play structure a "Six Pack." That makes six basic plays that can be run to both sides, thus doubling the number of plays without doubling the learning. They form the core structure of your attack. I believe the six plays should incorporate a straight-ahead dive up the middle, an off-tackle play, an outside play (a "sweep" for us), an outside end trap play that looks like a sweep, a counter play, and a reverse.

These six basic plays should be paired with an equal number of play action pass plays to complement the run and keep the defense honest. Don't get me wrong. We did not run only six plays in our games, but the core "Six Pack" of plays were our "go to" plays. We knew them inside and out, against any defense, stunt, or maneuver. This gave us confidence that no matter what new wrinkles were thrown at us in a key game, we could always run these plays. The deep confidence in these plays also helped to calm the jitters always present in the big game.

In going back to the basics, however, be careful not to oversimplify. I feel that is as wrong as trying to put in too much. Remember, this is an "upset" attempt. Your normal game won't beat the outstanding opponent. If they were not better than you are, it would not be an upset. When you add some "wrinkles" to your game, you let your team know that this game is special. New things that will help you win are always exciting to staff and players alike; your players will be more charged up for pre-game practice sessions. You also will give your opponents something to worry about and occupy their time during half time.

For an "upset" victory, you need every advantage you can get. Putting in something special for the game can give you the emotional edge, the strategic edge, and the element of surprise. Remember the Trojan War? When all else had failed for the Greeks in their attempt to topple the city of Troy, they pulled out all the stops. They went to the ultimate "trick play": the Trojan horse. The Greeks "set up" the Trojans. Just as in football, they feigned one way and countered back another. Odysseus was the quarterback of the best trick play in history!

One championship season we put in some new wrinkles that I borrowed from Mouse Davis' version of the "Run and Shoot" offense. We appropriately called the plays "Special Right" or "Special Left," "Special Right Pull" or "Special Left Pull," and "Special Follow." The "Special Left Pull" play was even written up in a national publication (*Football's Best Offensive Playbook*, by Dwight "Dee" Hawkes). The naming of these plays was intentional. They were "special" that day. They worked for us, and they worked well.

One coaching note on adding plays to your game: sometimes a good strategy is to use the special formation or trick play immediately before half time, or keep it only for the second half. The rationale is simple. Sometimes I liked to run the play right before half time, hoping that the opposition would spend their half-time preparation making adjustments to this special formation or play; then I wouldn't even run it in the second half. The flip side to this is to save the play for the second half. That way your opponents cannot prepare half-time adjustments for something they have not seen. You make the call. Both strategies are effective.

To this day I think the fun we had in putting in those simple extra plays helped us to enjoy our preparation for the big games. It also gave us confidence, which was exactly what we needed. Don't overlook these points.

Critical well-planned changes to your special teams can also provide an advantage. Never make wholesale changes, but a special maneuver to rush a punt or to block a field goal or extra point can produce great results. I can't recall the last time we went into a big game without some type of "trick" or "special" play. Do you want to enjoy the fruits of your labor? Do it the old fashioned way, but always have something special tucked away and ready to go. You just never know when you'll need it.

To prove my point, I could tell you about the game between the Division III Trinity Tigers and the Milsaps Majors, played on October 27, 2007 at Harper Davis Field in Jackson, Mississippi. The Tigers used fifteen laterals (that's right, 15) on the last play of the game to win 28-24. The play, dubbed by media as the "Mississippi Miracle," took over a minute to complete and secured the Southern Collegiate Athletic Conference championship for the Trinity Tigers. But really, I don't have to look any further back than Boise State vs. Oklahoma in the 2007 Fiesta Bowl. That was quite a show!

CONTROLLED FLEXIBILITY

In the preceding chapter on the game plan and play calling, I have stressed going back to basics and staying the course. I also pointed out that putting in new "wrinkles" can be advantageous. The two approaches can exist together. To be successful on big game days, you have to have what I call a "controlled flexibility" with your game plan. I know too many coaches who abandon their game plan far too early. Sometimes it takes time for things to start working. I know of too many other coaches, however, who never deviate from their original game plan even when it doesn't work at all. Both are wrong. Changing too quickly can be just as deadly as waiting too long to make a change.

Being too stubborn or proud to change can hurt you. Stephen R. Covey, in *The Seven Habits of Highly Effective People*, illustrates this point very well with a story told by Frank Koch in *Proceedings*, the magazine of the Naval Institute:

> Two battleships assigned to the training squadron had been at sea on maneuvers in heavy weather for several days. I was serving on the lead battleship and was on watch on the bridge as night fell. The visibility was poor with patchy fog,

so the Captain remained on the bridge keeping an eye on all activities. Shortly after dark, the lookout on the wing of the bridge reported, "Light bearing on the starboard bow." "Is it steady or moving astern?" the Captain called out.

The lookout replied, "Steady, Captain," which meant we were on a dangerous collision course with that ship.

The Captain then called to the signalman, "Signal that ship: we are on a collision course, advise you change course 20 degrees."

Back came a signal, "Advisable for you to change course 20 degrees."

The Captain said, "Send, I'm a captain, change course 20 degrees."

"I'm a Seaman second class," came the reply. "You had better change course 20 degrees."

By that time, the Captain was furious. He spat out, "Send, I'm a battleship. Change course 20 degrees."

Back came the flashing light, "I'm a lighthouse." We changed course.

Always remember the old adage, "You can't change the direction of the wind, but you can adjust the sails." Don't let pride stop you from making the adjustments and changes necessary to give your team the opportunity to win.

Sometimes, however, sticking with your original course works! Bronko Nagurski was once said to have scored a rather unusual touchdown. He ran through the entire defense. Players literally bounced off his body because of his battering-ram style of running. The last hit he took was after he had crossed the goal line. Actually, the last hit was made by his collision with the brick wall in Wrigley Field (he put a crack in the wall). When he returned to the sideline, he told Coach George Halas, "That last guy gave me quite a lick!" This story is part of early professional football lore. There is no verifiable author to give this story authenticity but that doesn't matter. It serves to illustrate the "full steam ahead" and "don't alter course" approach to football that some players and coaches follow. Bronko should have changed course, but that was not his "game plan." For him, it worked, but it won't work for everyone.

Knowing when to alter course and when to stay the course, as you can see, is critical. As a coach you have to be ready for all contingencies. When you alter course, have a plan ready. It must be a rehearsed adjustment to what the other team is throwing at you. You can't just draw plays in the dirt—well, sometimes maybe you can. When you stay the course, make sure your players are on the same mental page as you are. They must believe that if they keep hammering away, they will eventually break through.

We always preached that our conditioning would be the deciding factor. We would just wear our opponent down. Our players greeted the fourth quarter with four fingers in the air, chanting, "Fourth quarter, fourth quarter." We also had a precision movement at the end of the first and third quarters. We formed a running line from our huddle to the hash marks. In single file we trotted to the hash mark, planted our foot, and made a sharp turn to switch field position for the new quarter. We wanted to convey at all times that we were organized, united, and ready to go. We also had our quarterback or signal-calling linebacker run close to the sideline for some on-the-run instructions. When other teams were getting tired, we showed that we were still disciplined and under control.

I loved watching our team run along the sideline hash mark nearest our bench with their four fingers in the air chanting in rhythm, "Fourth quarter." It was our trigger to take control of the game. If we were ahead, it meant that we had to "keep the pedal to the metal." If we were behind, it meant "rally time." It was our way of telling our opponent, and ourselves, that the fourth quarter belonged to us! We were the team in control.

Overtime is another situation that calls for "controlled flexibility." You and your team must know exactly what you are going to do if you are involved in an overtime game. You should have a sequence of plays and strategy already in place for that event. Your plans should not be set in stone, however. Sometimes, certain plays have been going well during the course of the regular game. You may want to stick with those plays in overtime. However, to have your team confident and knowledgeable on how to run a specific sequence of plays will pay great dividends.

As far as overtime strategy goes, the flip of the coin will determine who gets to choose offense or defense. My preference was always to go on defense first. That way when we got our shot we knew exactly what we had to do. I also wanted to know when faced with a crucial play call what my quarterback's favorite pass play was. I wanted to know what my linemen's favorite play was in a crucial fourth-and-one call as well. I knew the answers to those questions before the game. Armed with that knowledge, I would usually call those very plays, knowing that they had the ultimate confidence in them. However, sometimes I called a time-out and asked them what they wanted to run. I didn't do that too often because every quarterback wanted to throw the ball, and every runner wanted his number called. I found that it was more effective when I said something like this: "I want to run a wedge play. I know it will work. But what I want most to know is, do you think you can make it work?"

Remember, their confidence will be the critical element. Their response was almost always, "Run it Coach, we can do it."

I'm convinced that in the ultimate analysis of a game won or lost, it won't boil down to your game plan or the selection of plays as the determining factor. I am not diminishing the importance of a strong and well thought-out game plan. It is important, but not as important as the team's belief in the coaches and the plan.

I've witnessed many a game in which the play calling was blamed for the loss. Sometimes that allegation has merit, but we never let our team fall into that way of thinking. I always gave them this scenario to drive home the point: there is no time on the clock, and we are on our own one-yard line, behind by six points. As the coach, I send a quarterback wedge play in as the last play attempt to win the game. I then asked my team, "What would you do? How would you react?"

If any player (it only takes one) thought that it was the dumbest call he had ever heard of, the play would be doomed from the start. But what if every player blocked his man and hustled downfield for a second block? Then the play would have a great chance of succeeding. I would assure the team that I would never call a quarterback wedge play in that situation. My hope was that our players would see the lesson in all of this. No matter what is called, if your players believe in the call and execute it to the best of their ability, it has a chance to succeed.

I've never seen an offensive play drawn up on the board that failed to score. Each play in our arsenal was designed to score from anywhere and at any time if executed perfectly. I believe the best game plan is one that has the following ingredients: great care and planning based on a strong scouting report, controlled flexibility that allows for rehearsed adjustments to react to the opponent's tactics, and the full confidence of the staff and team.

ACHIEVING COME-FROM-BEHIND WINS

How do you get a team to respond to being behind at half time of a game? The preparation for this situation is critical. If you want to have a successful season, you have to recognize that on average even the best teams will find themselves behind at half time at least two or three times in the course of a ten- or eleven-game regular season. If you are in the playoffs and seeking a state championship, that number will usually rise.

The ability to overcome a poor first half of play is essential to the upset. The team you are trailing could be either inferior or superior to your own team in the overall scheme of things. The challenge is to find the will not to quit or become disheartened when you find yourself behind a superior team. Confidence is much easier to find when you know you are better, but when you are clearly the underdog and find yourself behind late in a game, it is all too easy to believe the pre-game predictions that you will lose. Many teams will play to the level of that expectation.

How do you reverse this? How do a coach and his team prepare for the inevitable game where you are playing catch-up football? The answer is both simple and complex, but definitely achievable. First, it begins in the weight room and in the conditioning portion of every practice. The coach must instill in his players the knowledge that they have out-worked their opponent. When you know that you have already paid the higher price (the "blood, sweat and tears"), it becomes harder to quit. The team has to believe that their conditioning will eventually wear down the opponent. They must "keep the pedal to the metal" for the entire game. The relentless pressure of the attack will create the opportunities for success. Your players must stay focused and take advantage of the opportunities when they come. That is the key to the quiet confidence displayed by teams who believe that they are prepared and deserving of the win.

In order to set the climate in which our team could come from behind and win a big game, we prepared them mentally ahead of time. We always told them that even undefeated teams will find themselves behind at half time at least one or two times during the course of a season. When that did occur, we were mentally ready to accept it. It was not a surprise or shock for us. We took it in stride and knew that we would come from behind and win.

The coach has a critical part to play in pulling off the come-from-behind win. During the course of a game, but especially at the end of the half or end of the game, a coach has only split seconds to make decisions that will affect the outcome. The pressure of those situations can sometimes be overwhelming. Do we go for it on fourth and one, or do we punt? Do we kick the field goal or go for the touchdown? Do we go for a one-point conversion or a two-point conversion after the touchdown? All of these are high-stakes and high-pressure decisions that do not allow for protracted thought. You must make the decision quickly and decisively.

The thinking should take place prior to the game. In your preparation for the game, you should consider every situation that your team could encounter. Have your responses ready and rehearsed. The pre-game analysis will reassure your squad. They will know how to respond and will do so without panic or fear. The calm player is loose and ready to react and respond quickly and aggressively. Conversely, hesitation brings indecision, and indecision in football brings about confusion and doubt. Doubt will always translate into a lack of confidence and uninspired play.

To coach effectively, you must mask your own fears, uncertainties, and disappointments. This is especially important when you find yourself near the end of the game and still behind. Your face and your demeanor cannot reveal a sense of hopelessness to your players, but your feelings must be genuine. That's why you need a plan for an "Emotional Hail Mary."

A "Hail Mary" is a play used at the end of the half or game to pull a game out of the fire. An "Emotional Hail Mary" is a mindset, a feeling, and an emotional response that you call upon in order to make the "Hail Mary" work. You must have already programmed into yourself and your players a response to the negative situation: "This is how we will handle this obstacle and turn it into a positive. Until that final whistle blows I want 100% concentration and effort on getting one first down, then 2.5 yards at a time for 4 downs. We'll do this with no false starts, no missed assignments, and no fumbles. If we get that, then we will repeat that goal to get another first down. One by one, like climbing a ladder one rung at a time. No panic, just a grinding and dogged determination to make something happen one small step at a time. No matter what the score or the time on the clock, we will do what we know how to do best and we will do that to the best of our ability. If we go down, we will go down fighting and with our heads held high with pride and the satisfaction of knowing that we gave our all, every man, every play. Our effort will define our success–not the score. The score may reflect that we ran into a better opponent, but not necessarily the better team in terms of courage, hustle, never-quit attitude, and within the strictest parameters of great sportsmanship."

I also think that teams need a steady diet of inspiration. Show the films, read the articles, and tell your players the stories of past come-from-behind victories. Let them know that nothing excites people more than a team that perseveres and fights back. They will remember the team that never quits and pulls victory from the "jaws of defeat." Start in the off-season and feed your players a steady diet of illustration after illustration of athletes and teams who saw the potential disaster as an opportunity for their ultimate victory. Young athletes crave recognition of their efforts. Make them want it for themselves. Let them know that they will become part of the history of come-from-behind victories and upsets that will be passed down from future team to team. If yours is a new program, let your players know that they are beginning a new tradition that will become the bedrock of future success for their school. Let them also know that they are laying the foundation of success for their lives as well.

There are several great examples of fantastic and record-setting come-from-behind wins. In college football, the Division I-A record was shared for many years by two teams: Maryland and Ohio State. In the Maryland vs. Miami game in 1984 and the Ohio State vs. Minnesota game in 1989, both teams were able to overcome 31-point deficits and win their respective games. Maryland beat Miami 42-40 in the Orange Bowl against Bernie Kosar, and Ohio State beat Minnesota 41-37.

That was the standard until the 2006 football comeback game of all time in Division I-A history. Michigan State had just lost four games in a row and was trailing Northwestern 38-3 with 9:54 left to go in the third quarter. Can you believe a 35-point deficit late in the third quarter? Michigan State, through a combination of recovered fumbles, interceptions, blocked kicks, and inspired play, roared back to claim a miraculous victory by a score of 41-38.

Another great comeback story is the 1992 Buffalo Bills playoff win over the Houston Oilers. This game has been called the greatest comeback in NFL history. An injury to starting quarterback Jim Kelly brought Frank "Comeback" Reich into the game. Trailing 35-6, Reich led the Bills on a 35-3 scoring run in the second half and overtime. The result was a stunning 41-38 come-from-behind win. What makes this particularly interesting for me is the fact that this is the same quarterback, Frank Reich, that led the Maryland Terrapins to their great comeback win against Miami in 1984. Reich should forever be remembered as the "King" of comeback-quarterbacks.

Our players knew the stories of our own team's comebacks, and they knew the history of many of the famous historical college and pro comebacks. The knowledge that many others (including ourselves) had done it before gave us confidence that we too could do it. We could be the team that people would remember. I think that Frank Reich was able to win the game for the Buffalo Bills because he knew that he could. He had been there before.

Crowds emote the loudest when teams that have been down fight tenaciously to come back. There is something about us that gets us excited beyond all measure when a team fights back through adversity to win, overcomes some great challenge, or refuses to quit. There are literally hundreds of examples you can use as illustrations. My advice is for you to find the ones that best suit your situation, tell them to your team, and tell them often. Make the upset wins part of their memory bank. Your players will draw inspiration and confidence from these stories. They will also want to write their own "upset" story and become a part of the "upset" lore.

REVENGE

When you are looking for ways to fire up your players, you might be tempted to use revenge as motivation. Resist the temptation. Don't ever have your team play for revenge. It may work some of the time, but not most of the time. It is more a distraction than a motivational help. You and your players will become focused on individual players and coaches rather than the game, the formations, and the plays. When your own focus is compromised in this way, your team's focus is fragmented at best. That leaves no one totally free to read, react, and play with confidence and controlled abandon.

You have to be loose to win. Revenge-motivated play is counterproductive. Revenge is anger-driven, and anger is usually blinding. In other words, it hurts you more than your opponent. Dr. Lewis Smedes, a leading theologian, says in his book *Forgive and Forget: Healing the Hurts We Don't Deserve*, "The problem with revenge is that it never gets what it wants; it never evens the score. Fairness never comes. The chain reaction set off by every act of vengeance always takes its unhindered course." He also says, "To forgive is to set a prisoner free and discover that the prisoner was you."

In football, I equate forgiving with "moving on." When you've been wronged in the past (through unsportsmanlike play, having the score run up on you, negative comments in the paper, etc.) you and your team cannot dwell on it, but instead should move on. Once removed from the constraints of false motivation through revenge, your players and coaches can be completely free to focus on the task at hand and the game. I have witnessed players who thought themselves wronged in games go headhunting for the alleged perpetrator. Their desire for revenge usually cost their team an unsportsmanlike penalty, and in extreme cases, resulted in ejection from the game.

There is no focus on the objective of the game when revenge takes center stage and becomes the focal point of our actions. I have experienced this personally. We were losing a tight game late in the fourth quarter. We had already had several touchdowns and long runs called back on what I felt were not good calls. I was frustrated. Then we got a break and scored the go-ahead touchdown. It would have been the winning touchdown if I had not let revenge and anger overcome my judgment. We kicked off after the touchdown, and on our opponent's next possession we intercepted the ball deep in their territory. I was still upset over those calls. My offensive end coach, Dave Taylor, walked up to me and said, "You're going to sit on it now, aren't you, Coach?" He meant, "Run out the clock — we have the game won."

After many years I still remember this as if it were yesterday. I told Dave that I would, but first I wanted to run the same play that had been called back for touchdowns several times already. I told him, "I'll run out the clock after this last play." I wanted to score one more touchdown! You can finish the story; I know you know the result! We ran the play, but fumbled the ball on one bounce to their streaking defensive end. Sixty-five yards later he and his team were celebrating a touchdown and a win!

I learned a valuable lesson the hard way that day. The negative emotions generated by the desire for revenge must be harnessed by the coach and redirected into a positive approach to the game. Eradicate revenge motivation from yourself and your team. Instead, unleash a laser-sharp focus and surge mentality and watch them meld together to produce superior results. You must preach and preach *ad nausea* to get this point across to your team, but after your players do grasp this concept, amazing things start to happen. They will play harder and smarter; they will be more focused and more physical. You, as a coach, will be smarter and more focused as well. "Cool under fire" is a key ingredient to good coaching and playing. Without it, the dream of the upset stays only a dream.

There is a side benefit to this approach, as well. With your guidance your team will also strive to play under the strictest rules of good sportsmanship. It is a lost art for some teams these days, but an art that must be taught and practiced to preserve the integrity of our game.

I have just shared with you how my own desire for revenge resulted in dire results for our team. The experience reinforced for me the notion that games are more often "lost" than "not won." Many people think that games are won by outstanding plays. Sometimes that is true, but my experience and observation tell me that defeats are more often "snatched from the jaws of victory" because of the following list of major contributors: turnovers (fumbles, interceptions), lack of discipline, lack of focus, penalties (and the loss of composure that usually follows), tentative play (playing not to lose instead of playing to win), panicking and not staying with the game plan long enough, or stubbornly holding onto a game plan that simply isn't working.

To win the big games, a coach needs to prepare himself, his staff, and his team to deal with these negative factors. Parents and fans can also be enlisted to help your team handle these difficult situations. If they know your philosophy about turning negatives into positives, they can better react and reinforce your efforts. You need to have them all on board (though it will never be 100%) to achieve the ultimate success. They will be behind you if you make it a priority.

Your team is the most important part of this equation. You must develop within them a trust and a faith in you and your staff. To paraphrase the inspirational scholar and writer Stephen Kuusisto: Their faith will move from belief into conviction, then to certainty.

TEAM AS FAMILY

Crucial to our team philosophy was that we were family. Everyone says that, but do they really practice what they preach? I tried to be as faithful to the family concept as I could. I inherited one of my primary beliefs from my coaching mentor, Bill L. Cole. I maintained his philosophy that we never cut anyone who came out for the team. As long as a player followed our rules and was true to the program, he was a permanent part of our team. I realize that for some large schools and programs with budget restrictions, this might not be possible, but if you can, I strongly recommend that you follow this policy.

The other thing that I believed, however, might not be endorsed by all. A player who violated team rules was not automatically expelled from the program. There were exceptions to this policy; however, whenever there was no conflict with other school or district rules, I always tried to keep the player with us. My thinking was simple: how can you help someone if you separate him from the scope of your influence – your daily interaction? If your team is truly a family, consequences must be administered, but these consequences need not necessarily result in expulsion from the team/family.

If I suspected that a player was "partying" and possibly drinking, I had a plan of attack. My friend Tom Harrison was a guidance counselor at our school. He had been an All-State football player and had played on one of the University of Delaware's undefeated teams. He also worked with Alcoholics Anonymous as a counselor in the prisons. After meeting with the suspected offender, I sent the young man directly to Tom, and he took over. If the player had a problem, Tom made sure that he was put back on the proper track and that he received the counseling and support that he needed to beat the disease. If he was just partying or experimenting, then Tom and I would double hit him with the consequences of his actions. We would give him a second chance, but he had to stop *now*. If he refused to change his ways, he was voluntarily choosing to remove himself from our team.

We followed this course without the knowledge of anyone other than the parents. You as a coach have to be careful: make sure that you are not violating any school or district policies. I took this approach with players that I suspected were heading for trouble. There were some offenders who were caught outright, and school district policy had to take precedence. You cannot put yourself in a situation that conflicts with your own school and district rules. Loyalty to your school and its rules is just as important as your insistence that your players follow the rules of the team. Tom and I wanted our players to remain in an environment that would be conducive to a change of attitude and behavior.

Some of our players did not have good role models at home. I wanted our team family to fill that void. I reprimanded a player severely once for not showing up for a game. He was a JV player who had worked hard and deserved to have the opportunity to suit up for the varsity games. When he didn't show up for the game, I was angry.

The young man told me he had not been able to get a ride. That wasn't good enough for me. I told him he'd better be at the next game, or that would be his last opportunity to suit for the varsity game.

The next week I looked out the window of our locker room and saw the player getting out of a taxicab. He had scraped up the money for the cab because no one at home would take him to the games. The money for the cab ride was a significant sacrifice for that young man. I felt terrible about the situation, and after reimbursing him for the taxi, I made sure that he had a ride with one of our players each week after that.

Your recognition of a problem and follow-up intervention could prove to be life-changing for a player in a crisis situation. On one occasion, we intervened at the bus station to prevent a player from running away from home. Another player confided to me that he was involved as a lookout for local drug pushers. I told him that had to stop immediately. His answer was that it was the only way he could pay for his football shoes. We made sure that he had shoes from that point on. This same young man went on to obtain his college degree and is now a highly respected member of our community. We are most proud of the fact, however, that he has dedicated his life to helping others escape the life style of despair that he had experienced himself. Your actions will speak louder than your words. Don't just talk family; be ready to back up the talk with action, and don't limit your attention to the "stars" of the team. Ninety percent of the time our "family" interventions involved non-starting players. Help and support was provided for all of our young men, not just the most talented ones.

Your players can also support each other in meeting the challenges facing young people today. One of the most successful things we did to try to build team unity and offer guidance to our players occurred during our undefeated state championship season of 1995. That year *USA Today* ranked our team as one of the top teams in the nation. We had great leadership. I asked our seniors to make a list of things they thought would be important to pass on to the younger players. We brainstormed together and came up with a list of topics for discussion. The list ran the gamut from A to Z. Each senior selected a topic to present to the rest of the team. Two of our team leaders, Jeff Hockenbrock and Rahsaan Matthews, were particularly outstanding. Jeff went on to star at Yale, and Rahsaan became the all-time career passing record holder for Delaware State University. Under their leadership and direction, the seniors gave their perspectives on how to handle every conceivable situation that a young man could encounter in today's world. They talked about drugs, drinking, dating, peer pressure, loyalty, homework, parent relationships, divorce—you name it! The kitchen sink was not spared. To this day I am in awe of how they shared their feelings with the younger players. I was equally impressed with the response that I witnessed from the underclassmen. You could have heard a pin drop.

My staff has often commented that it is unfortunate that we did not videotape or record the session in some fashion. I thought at the time that it would inhibit the speakers. Looking back now, I realize that nothing would have intimidated that group of seniors. I am positive that the experience left an indelible impression and impact on all their lives and on mine as well.

I always thought and taught that our program was more about teaching young men how to become productive members of the community than becoming good football players. Guess what? They work together. The payoff is tremendous. The dedicated, honest, loyal, ethical, play-by-the-rules person will carry over those same qualities into his football. He will be loyal, dedicated, and have a work ethic that will lead him to become a better football player. He will also better grasp the importance of sportsmanship: play hard, but play by the rules with respect for your opponent.

The team as a whole benefits from this attitude. The dedicated, ethical player will be a better follower and ultimately a better leader. He will assist the younger and the weaker teammates to help them win, and in so doing he wins also. That is the essence of a true "win-win" philosophy. That is the type of player that I want on my team: "All for one and one for all."

COLLECTIVE RESPONSIBILITY AND "WIN-WIN"

We always felt it was important to set up as many practice situations as we could to allow our players to experience doing things that they weren't sure that they could do. We also knew that we had to inspire them to play for more than just themselves. We wanted their individual success to be a part of our team success. We wanted them to know that we win and we lose together. It is not enough for one player to be successful. It is the responsibility of every player to see that each and every teammate succeeds as well. When one fails, we all fail together. It is what Duke's Mike Krzyzewski calls "collective responsibility."

We engineered situations that would allow our players to discover this concept of interdependence for themselves. One way was through our sprints at the end of practice. We put our players in their stances and varied our cadence to set them off on 40-yard sprints. If one player jumped, the whole team had to back up five yards and run the sprint again at the longer distance. Many players at first thought this was unfair. They didn't jump, so why should they have to run the extra and longer sprint? The answer is simple. In a game, when one player jumps offside or is called for an illegal procedure, the whole team is backed up five yards. Only one is guilty, but all are punished. When the same scenario is applied in a practice situation, the protesting players will soon understand the point and real leadership begins to take over. The players aren't very happy with the offender. They will begin to "work" on him to mend his ways. If done properly and monitored by the coaches, this method will produce positive results. Be vigilant that this does not get out of hand, however. You must instruct the team on how to help their teammate become more focused in a positive way. In our experience, this technique does work. We always wanted to be the least penalized team in the game, and we usually were.

We coupled the "collective responsibility" concept with the "win-win" philosophy. We wanted our players to understand that it was not enough to improve themselves alone. We wanted them to help their teammates improve as well. It makes sense even on a self-ish level. We wanted our players' thinking to be like this: If I am a starter, how will I improve on a daily basis? I have to work against a blocking or tackling partner every day in drill-time. In team-time I have to go against the "thud" or practice team. If that practice partner works hard every day and improves his game, he will push me harder and harder. That daily struggle will force me to improve. It would then be in my best interest to help that player improve. His improvement will be my gain and the team's gain. In other words, if he wins, I win, and the team wins as well.

Several other benefits will result when the "win-win" philosophy is applied. If we lose a starter due to injury, discipline, or academics, then an improved back-up player will be able to step in and maintain a high level of play. This actually played out on the field in our first state championship win in 1982. We lost what would have been a first team All-State middle-guard right before the play-offs. The senior back-up player, who had seen only reserved playing time during the year, stepped into the starting role. His name was José Baez – I'll never forget him! He was a full-of-life, high-energy player who had accepted his role all year without complaint. In the state championship game, his play was so exceptional that he was voted the most valuable lineman of the game by a local radio station. I am convinced that his personal success was a direct by-product of our "win-win" approach and total team concept.

Well-trained back-up players will also better prepare the starting players for the speed, skill, and execution level of their opponents. Many of these players will be younger players who will, as a result, be better prepared to assume starting roles the next year.

Also, never underestimate the improvement in morale that this approach creates. When your team finally discovers and understands the concept of "collective responsibility" coupled with the "win-win" philosophy, they will be ready to take on the challenge of pulling off the upset together as one – a team. As a result, they will not play selfishly; they will play for the team. The process of self-discovery becomes the fuel that ignites a burning desire to excel. Kurt Hahn, the founder of the "Outward Bound" program, summed it up very well: "Self discovery is the end product of a great challenge mastered, when the mind commands the body to do the seemingly impossible, when courage and strength are summoned to extraordinary limits for the sake of something outside the self."

BUILDING TEAM-SYNERGY

No one thing prepares your team to win the big games. It is an accumulation of many small things woven together over time that does it. In his book *Leading with the Heart*, Coach Mike Krzyzewski of Duke University illustrates the analogy of the "fist." No one individual can do it alone. It takes the entire team to produce a consistent winner. One finger can be easily broken, but when all fingers are joined together and formed into a fist, they are unbreakable. For "Coach K" the five fingers represent communication, trust, collective responsibility, caring and pride. He says, "The fist is a great metaphor." As *Wall Street Journal* writer Thaddeus Herrick explains it, "In Mr. Krzyzewski's eyes, five less talented players who come together as a team can beat five more talented players who don't."

I demonstrated this point to my own teams using a "hands-on" technique. I took a pencil and showed how easy it was to break. Then I put a whole bunch of pencils together bound by a rubber band. The first time I did this some of the outer pencils broke. The illustration wasn't as effective as I had hoped; plus, it was costly – I had to replace the pencils I had borrowed from the office. I now use Coach K's illustration of the fist to demonstrate the point. It works, and it's cheaper.

Upon reflection, maybe the pencil demonstration does work. Those outer pencils that broke could represent the players that have only marginally bought into the program. We don't need marginal players; we need everyone on board. Nature provides us with the same lesson. Did you know that geese fly in a "V" formation for a reason? The flapping wings of each goose in the formation create uplift for the others behind it. There is an estimated 71% more flying range for the birds in the "V" formation than there would be if each bird were on its own. Working together, they can accomplish so much more. By the way, next time you see a flock of geese flying in "V" formation, notice that one line of the "V" is always longer than the other. Do you know why one line is longer than the other? Because it has more birds in it! Sorry, I just couldn't pass up that one.

You can come up with your own way to illustrate this point. Remember, this is not a new concept. King Solomon, one of the wisest men who ever lived, had his own version of this principle. He said: "Two are better than one . . . though one may be overpowered by another, two can withstand him. And a threefold cord is not quickly broken" (*Ecclesiastes* 4.8-12). If two, five, nine, or eleven athletes (depending on your sport) all pull together, just think what could happen! What if everyone on the team right down to the student managers all pull together? What if they practice exactly what we preached: "Every one, every play"? The possibilities would be endless. Some call this "synergy." Look it up in the dictionary. *Webster's* defines "synergy" as ". . . the interaction of two or more agents or forces so that their combined effect is greater than the sum of their individual effects."

That sums it up well. To be successful, a team has to be like the Three Musketeers, "All for one and one for all." "Synergy" is the word, but we just called it "team." Abe Lincoln alluded to the same philosophy when he stated, "United we stand, divided we fall." So get your team to stand together like the "Fist." Their punch will be powerful!

TEAM, NOT SELF:
Synergy Illustrated

One of my most memorable experiences in coaching occurred when I had the opportunity to work with Coach Tubby Raymond of the University of Delaware. Tubby is a legendary Hall of Fame coach. In 1984, he gave me the opportunity to work with his team in spring ball. From that experience I gained an insight into a brilliant offensive and creative mind, but I learned other things even more valuable. I heard Tubby talking on the radio one time about coaches and their impact on a game. He said that he never publicly stated after a game that he had been out-coached. It sort of shocked me at first until I heard his explanation. He said that if you take sole credit for the losses, then are you not also taking credit for the wins? He wanted his entire team to be invested in the outcome of the game. It was their game to win and their game to lose *together*. He never wanted to take the credit, good or bad, away from his team. If they were to be successful, the players and coaches had to share the full responsibility. If they won, they won as a team. If they lost, they lost as a team.

I have been out-coached in games, but I took a page from Coach

Raymond on this. I only publicly spoke of our shared experience of winning or losing–staff and players together as a team. It was different in our closed private team meetings. I always pointed out my own correctable errors as well as the team's mistakes. I think there is great wisdom in this. Never single out a player as a reason for the loss or win, and never single out yourself. To do so is to miss a great teaching lesson for your team: There is no "I" in the word "Team." It is the difference between a "monergistic" vs. "synergistic" philosophy. In both words one finds the Greek root "erg," which means "work." But "mono" means "one." It takes a lot of work, but never just one person. It takes all working together to be successful. That's why our philosophy of team is plural and synergistic.

We used an illustration to help our players visualize this concept. In their notebooks and on the blackboard we displayed this illustration:

TEAM

ME

Translation: "Team" *over* "me"

It works the same way when you win. To single out the performance of one individual in a team sport is poor coaching. Let the newspaper writers do that, not you. Your goal is to promote harmony, unselfishness and team unity. To single out an individual is self-defeating. I was always disturbed when a player thought he was above the team. We constantly reminded players (particularly the backs and ends) that they couldn't accomplish anything without their teammates. How can a quarterback throw a touchdown without a center snapping him the ball correctly, an entire line blocking for him, and a receiver running a good pattern and catching the ball? It cannot be done alone.

We once had a back who was a good young man, but a bit full of himself. One day I took the team up to the game field. I put my starting defense on the ball on the twenty-yard line. I placed my one back five yards back, and I snapped the ball to him. My only instructions were for the defense to stop him (no piling on) and for him to try to score. That's it, pure and simple. You know the results! Four straight downs later, the back found himself with negative yardage. Each carry resulted in a major loss of yards. After practice, I followed up with the young man. I made sure that he understood why I did what I did and that I valued him as an individual and as a player. He just had to understand that he had to do his "individual best" within the context of the "team." I never had to deal with that problem again – lesson learned!

THE WEATHERVANE
AND THE HELMET

I was always looking for ways to motivate our team. I liked to use visual, hands-on illustrations whenever possible. Here are a couple that you might be able to integrate into your own repertoire of motivational devices. Make a weathervane – the standard type of weathervane you might see on top of a farmhouse out in the country. It should have a base with a swivel arrow that indicates the four points: North, East, South and West. Label the arrow with the word "Success," or whatever you prefer. If you make the arrow blade with a removable label section, you could change the label title to suit a particular game or subject for illustration. If you label the arrow blade with the word "Success," it makes for a great visual analogy.

Gather your team around you in a circle. Spin the weathervane. No matter where it ends up, it will still be pointing at your team. (That's why they are in a circle.) Tell your players, "No matter what happens in the game, no matter what obstacle gets thrown your way (from any direction), the 'arrow of success' will point your way."

The arrow will always point to your team. Sometimes you could say that it points to a particular member on your team. Then, the point is made to that individual team member that he may need to step up and deliver something special that day. The beauty of this is that the arrow, if spun multiple times, will point to both starters and non-starters. It doesn't make any difference. Each person on the team, regardless of position or playing status, has a role—and that role could be the difference between winning and losing. The arrow will sometimes point to an individual, but it *always* points to the team. Any one player is always contributing within the framework (the circle) of the team.

No matter which way the "winds of fate" may blow, this team will be successful. North winds can be harsh (penalties, fumbles, interceptions, bad calls etc.) but the arrow of success will always point to your team. Southern winds can be helpful (you'll get your share of good breaks, but you have to capitalize on them). Eastern and western winds can buffet your team from side to side (bad things sometimes seem to come at you simultaneously from the left and the right), but still the arrow of success points in your direction.

The weathervane illustration is a great way to convey the idea to your team that no matter what happens, they can and will ride out the storm and achieve success. The removable label blade on the arrow will allow you to be inventive. You can put your opponent's team name there or provide other motivational words that mean something special to your players. Don't limit yourself or your team. They will be creative if you give them the opportunity. The bottom line is that you are converting their thoughts and energies into a positive state of mind. They will "buy in" to your idea and adopt it as their own: no matter what happens in the game they will be successful.

You can define "success" any way you want. If you are going for the upset win, then define it as such. If you have a young and "green" squad, your definition of success may be a set number of first downs or yards that your players make or give up. Whatever the goal, define it, work toward it, and let nothing deter you and your team from achieving it.

As a follow-up you could make a miniature spin card from firm stock paper or cardboard. Label the card any way you want. Cut out a hole in the middle of the card and place a paper fastener with the double prongs in the hole. Place a spin arrow in the middle attached to the fastener. In a team meeting have your players spin the arrow and read what the arrow points to. Ask them to tell you and the team what their take is on the word: what does it mean to them? You can use all kinds of motivational words or sayings surrounding the spin arrow. I took a drawing of our helmet and made a motivational word page. I randomly placed the words all around the helmet picture. I placed the words around a helmet on purpose. The helmet was the closest thing to their head, and that was where I wanted these words to go—inside the helmet and into their minds. I used words and phrases such as "Hustle," "Never Quit," "Intensity," "Surge," "Swarm," "Pride," "Focus," "Desire," "Passion," "Sacrifice," "Team" and "HAM" (Hostile, Agile, Mobile), to name a few. These words were constant reminders of our football philosophy and how we wanted them to play the game.

You can also use these words with the spinner. Every time the arrow is given a spin, it will point to something special. Each week the list can change. Keep the spin arrow and fastener, but use a different background sheet. Each team you play has a different set of emphasis points for the week. You could use this as a supplement to your weekly scouting reports. It also will re-emphasize for your players the keys for the upcoming game.

Anything that can help your players visualize the cornerstones of your program and repetitively reinforce your goals is a must-have and must-do proposition!

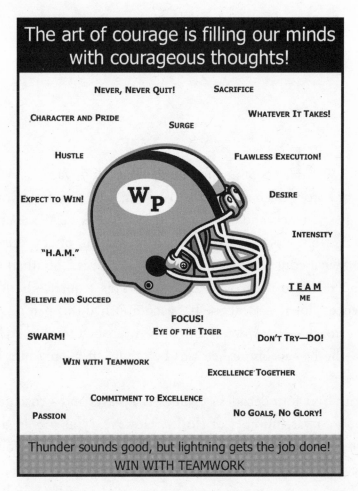

ON MOTIVATION

I recommend this rule for motivation: give your players one story from a past famous event, one story from your own personal experience, and one from their own recent experience. I find that going from global to personal works best and offers your team a vision of what could be. In other words, "think big," but then personalize and relate to their own experience. This sequence builds their confidence: global – someone has accomplished this before; personal to the coach – you have accomplished this before; personal to the player – he has accomplished this before (even if only in a limited way).

With over four decades of games as a player and a coach, I could draw upon a vast number of stories. However, you should use anything that you can that is relevant and "present tense" for your players. Recall a scrimmage, or even a play in a game in which they fought hard. When I was a young coach, I once used a twelve-minute quarter of a game in which we were soundly defeated. In that one quarter, however, we held our opponent scoreless, and we out-gained them on the ground and in the air. We also had a goal line stand. We lost by over thirty points, but I concentrated only on that one quarter and used it to provide inspiration. We played with pride and a "never quit" attitude during that quarter.

Show your team that they can do it and that they have done it, if only briefly. All you ask for is the sustained effort: what you know you can do and have done for one quarter, try to now do for four quarters. You can always find some bright spot in a recent game or scrimmage to illustrate this point.

Also, give them small goals if you are overmatched. To accomplish this, I would take them to the game field and show them physically what 2.5 yards looks like. I asked them to just give us 2.5 yards every play. Walk it off for them. It is easy to illustrate that if you can just get 2.5 yards per down, it starts to add up. Two and a half yards plus 4 downs equal ten yards–a first down! That's all you need. Two to four first downs and you are across midfield, and then three to five more and you can kick a field goal or score a touchdown. I never wanted them to think that they had to go eighty yards or more to score, just 2.5 yards, one yard at a time.

Joe Torre, in his book *Joe Torre's Ground Rules for Winners*, says, "Think of winning as a puzzle. To achieve a 'big' goal, assemble a large number of little accomplishments and make them fit perfectly together." This illustrates our philosophy exactly. He adds, "Don't focus on winning . . . concentrate so completely on the small bites that you'll need someone to tell you that you've achieved a victory." Our goals always reflected the micro to macro or "small to big" principle.

A good "life" story to illustrate this point comes from famed author and correspondent Eric Sevareid. David J. Schwartz, in his book *The Magic of Thinking Big*, recounts Sevareid's story in his own words:

During World War II, I and several others had to parachute from a crippled army transport plane into the mountainous jungle on the Burma-India border. It was several weeks before a relief expedition could reach us, and then we began a painful plodding march out to civilized India. We were faced by a 140-mile trek, over mountains, in August heat and monsoon rains.

In the first hour of the march I rammed a boot nail deep into one foot; by evening I had bleeding blisters the size of a 50-cent piece on both feet. Could I hobble 140 miles? Could the others, some in worse shape than I, complete such a distance? We were convinced we could not. But we could hobble to that ridge, we could make the next friendly village for the night. And that, of course, was all we had to do . . .

Eric Sevareid called this the principal of the "next mile." Concentrate first on the small things, the little details, and they together will give you the "bigger" results. This simple approach works wonders.

I should, however, caution you that you should carefully choose your illustrations.

Make sure they will have the desired effect on your team. Never forget the old coach who was trying to teach his team about the effects of alcohol. He assembled the team in front of him and set out two beakers filled with liquid. He explained to the team that one of the jars was filled with water and the other with alcohol. He then proceeded to take a large earthworm out of a third jar and placed it into the water-filled jar. The earthworm swam around in the water with no ill effect. He then placed the worm into the jar filled with alcohol. The worm immediately began to struggle and then ceased to move. The coach savored the moment and asked the team what lesson they had just learned. One of the backs raised his hand and said, "Great illustration Coach, I get it! If we drink alcohol we won't get worms!"

Never assume you are being understood as you intend. (Author's note to all line coaches: notice my use of a "back" in this story. This one's for you. This story was originally told with a "big tackle" as the fall guy).

Not every "gimmick" or motivational device works for all teams. I know this from experience. When I was a young coach, I read a story about the legendary Bud Wilkinson of Oklahoma. Coach Wilkinson was always one of my favorite coaches and role models. After all, it was Coach Wilkinson who coached the Philadelphia Eagles' Tommy McDonald while he was at the University of Oklahoma. I had the pleasure of meeting him and Duffy Dougherty of Michigan at their 1981 Coach of the Year Clinic in Washington, D.C. (I was there to accept the Coach of the Year award for Delaware on behalf of our coaches and team.) I read and gathered as much information on Coach Wilkinson's coaching career as I could get my hands on.

To say that I admired Wilkinson's coaching style would be an understatement. I have read that one day prior to a big game, he was so upset with his team that he sent them off the field. They had a decision to make. If they weren't going to practice well and hard, they weren't going to practice at all. The team headed for the showers, but then got together and begged the coach to let them go back out on the field. Coach Wilkinson relented, and his team had their most inspired practice of the year. Of course, they won the big game.

That story inspired me. One day we were practicing for our big game and the heavens opened upon us. A driving hard rain began pouring down. My team usually loved to practice in the rain, but that day they were all standing around, huddled like a herd of cows in a pasture. I was getting angry, but I had the solution – Bud Wilkinson! I called my captains over, and in front of the staff, I told them to go back and tell the rest of the team that they had a choice to make. They could go home right now. Practice was over; we were not getting anything positive accomplished practicing this way. Or, they could vote to stay and we'd supercharge the practice and get ourselves one step closer to winning the big game. As the captains huddled with the team, I grabbed the manager. I told him to set up the field for a scrimmage. We hardly ever scrimmaged live, and I knew that the team would love it, especially in the rain. The manager took off on the run to get the down marker and chains. The captains came running up to me to give me their answer.

As the captains approached, I thought: Now we're in business. I was so proud of this "brilliant" motivational tactic that I had engineered! The captains ran up and said without hesitation: "Coach, we've decided to go in!" I don't recall saying a word. I just stood there dumbfounded. The team ran off the field faster than they had run all day. I was in shock. My staff, however, thought that it was the funniest thing they had ever witnessed. To this day we still laugh about my great motivational ploy.

Is there a lesson in all of this? Absolutely! Know your players. Not every motivational technique works the same way on all teams. Furthermore, not every technique works on each individual player the same way. Experienced coaches can give you strategies for motivation; however, nothing beats knowing your own team and your individual players. Only you can develop your team's personalized motivational package because you know them best.

Never be afraid to try different things to motivate your team. How do you think the veteran coaches got to the point that they can give advice? If they are like me, they got there through trial and error. What worked last year might not work this year. The main thing is to keep trying until you find the right equation for your team. In other words, *never quit*!

ORDINARY TO EXTRAORDINARY:
Stories to Inspire

Your players will also benefit from hearing true-life examples of other "ordinary" people who have accomplished the seemingly impossible. I have often shared an incident I remember from my childhood that illustrates the point. A woman and child were trapped and pinned in an automobile following a terrible accident. The doors were damaged and jammed shut. The husband and father of the victims was nearby when the accident occurred. He raced over to the car, and with his bare hands literally took the door off its hinges to reach his loved ones. I remember my father telling me this story because it happened on the road less than a hundred yards from where we lived. An ordinary man did the impossible. Where did the strength come from? It had to come from within. He refused to be beaten by the obvious obstacles. He would not allow his wife and child to stay trapped. He acted on pure emotion, adrenalin and determination.

If these superhuman feats can and do happen, how can we harness that energy for a game? We might not be able to duplicate his feat; however, we can apply the principle of drawing from deep within ourselves to accomplish something that no one thinks we can accomplish. We need to learn how to tap into that power.

Another story that illustrates ordinary people doing extraordinary things is the story of a Georgetown University football player named Bill Carroway. James Jeffrey recounts this memorable story in the book *Courage to Conquer*. Lou Little, head coach of Georgetown University, received a visitor to his home the night before the last game of the season. The night visitor was Bill Carroway. Bill was a senior player who had never played in a game. When Coach Little opened the door, Bill said, "Coach, I've seen great teams go out on that field in my four years here, but I haven't had a chance to play. I was wondering if you'd give me that opportunity tomorrow, whether it be for one minute, or even one play – just let me get in the game." Coach Little told him that he couldn't promise anything. This game was too important to the team – it was for the conference championship – but he would do the best that he could.

The day of the game came, and as predicted, the game was close – right down to the wire. Georgetown was losing by three at the half, and the last minutes of the game still found them behind. Bill Carroway realized that his opportunity to play was slipping away with every tick of the clock. He began to pace up and down the sideline in front of Coach Little, hoping to be seen. The coach did see him. Thinking that he had nothing to lose, he decided to reward the young man for his four years of dedication and hard work to the program. He called Carroway's name and told him to go in at halfback. His first play from scrimmage resulted in a forty-yard run! The fans went crazy. They began to search the game roster and couldn't even find his name. It wasn't there. Who was this kid? With time literally running out they called one last "Hail Mary" into the end zone. The ball was heaved high into the air and as it came down, someone leaped higher than everyone else, caught the ball and fell into the end zone – touchdown! It was him – the boy who had never started a game in his life; the boy who begged to be put into the game. How could this be? He won the game!

After the game, the coach worked his way through the crowd back to the locker room. He went straight to the bench where Bill was sitting, taking off his uniform for the last time in his career. Coach Little asked him the obvious question: where did the inspiration come from? All season long Carroway had been just an average player. All of a sudden he asked to be put into the biggest game of the season, and he helped win the game – how? Bill looked Coach Little in the eye and told him:

"Coach, when I was born, my mother died, and all through the years my wonderful father wanted me to do two things. The first thing was to go to college and get an education. I've done that . . . The second thing my dad wanted me to do, Coach, was to play football. You see, I knew my dad would never see me play football because he was blind. Several days ago my dad died, and I knew that today would be the first and the last time he would ever have a chance to see me play. So you see, Coach, I had to succeed; there were no two ways about it for me, there was just one path."

For me this story is truly inspirational. This young man saw himself playing in the big game, and he saw his father watching him. He believed that he could play inspired football and help his team win. He also wanted to do it for his father, who had sacrificed and done so much for him. He did it! Remember Napoleon Hill: "Whatever the mind can conceive and believe, the mind can achieve."

I loved to tell my teams these amazing success stories. I wanted them to believe that they too could tap into this miraculous mindset and accomplish great things.

DAVE TIBERI – "MR. HUSTLE"

One of our best centers ever (and we always had great centers) was a young man named Dave Tiberi. At 165 pounds, he was not a big center, but he was tireless. On the break of the huddle he sprinted to the ball each and every time. He was like a machine. He became a First Team All-State center on our undefeated 1983 team.

Dave's story did not end there, however. In Delaware, the Tiberi family name is synonymous with great boxing. Almost all of Dave's siblings were great fighters and/or great boxing trainers. Dave compiled a 62-0 amateur boxing record and won two Pennsylvania Golden Glove Championships. He then turned to professional boxing, and through hard work and dedication moved up in the rankings.

In 1991, Dave became Delaware's first professional boxing champion with a fifth-round TKO win over Ed Hall. He became the IBC Super Welterweight Champ. With that win, Dave earned a title shot against the reigning IBF Champion, James Toney.

On February 8, 1992, in Atlantic City, New Jersey, Dave was ranked as an overwhelming underdog by those who didn't know him. The first round started the way many thought it would; he took a

161

hard right hook to the head, and many thought that would be the end for Dave. But just as he did when he played for us, he never quit and kept hustling. He gradually started to wear Toney down with his relentless energy. The fight progressed, and the crowd grew louder and louder as Dave began clearly to dominate. They sensed that the upset was definitely in the making.

To everyone who witnessed the bout, David was the clear winner, but two of the three judges awarded the winning decision to Toney. There was outrage in Delaware and across the nation. Delaware Senator Bill Roth even initiated a Senate investigation into boxing. Congress eventually responded by passing the Boxing Safety Act of 1997, aimed at cleaning up professional boxing.

In my mind and countless others, Dave Tiberi won that fight fair and square, but he was not rewarded for his efforts. I know that he won the bout on pure determination and "hustle." His skills were awesome, but his "never quit" attitude and "hustle" were the main ingredients for his success. I tell this story for many reasons. Dave Tiberi personifies "hustle." As a man of great faith, he also personifies the ability to take negative circumstances and turn them into positive ones. Dave has since left the boxing arena; however, he has taken the same "hustle factor" and turned it into an extremely successful media company, TNT Enterprises. He also opened the Dave Tiberi Youth Center, serving mostly disadvantaged youth. To me he is a true winner–a winner in boxing, yes, but even more, a winner in life.

BELIEVING — BUYING IN

When it comes to coaching your team to win, sometimes it just boils down to blind faith. It's like religion–you either believe, or you don't. You accept the tenets of your faith or you reject them. I choose to accept them. I can't explain all of them, and I can't prove all of them, but in my heart I know they are true.

Your relationship with your staff and team must be the same way. Sometimes you just have to believe in each other. Forget what seems obvious, forget what seems rational (forget the newspaper clippings predicting your defeat), forget what the "hallway warriors" say, and forget what everyone else thinks! Just believe in your coaches, your team, and yourself. We used to tell our players that if they would all "buy in," we would win.

Optimism is infectious, and it is the only route to success. Colin Powell once said, "Perpetual optimism is a force multiplier." Create the climate of optimism and watch it spread. We always followed up with this: "For those of you who don't believe yet, 'fake it' until you do!" And do it with great Dick Vitale-like enthusiasm and energy. As a matter of fact, I always wanted my players to always be "Vitale-like." To define this I created an acronym for "VITALE": **V**ery **I**ntense, **T**alking **A**nd **L**ooking **E**nthusiastic.

Journalist Daniel Schorr once said, "The secret of success is sincerity. Once you can fake that you've got it made." That's a comical take on our philosophy, but the point is that you have to be on the road to sincerity. We wanted our players to practice walking the walk and talking the talk until it eventually became a part of them. Our ultimate desire was to have a "DNA match," a match between our coaches, players, goals and philosophy.

We wanted all of us to be on the same page. Dale Carnegie, in *How to Win Friends and Influence People,* said, "Action seems to follow feeling, but really action and feeling go together; and by regulating the action, which is under the more direct control of the will, we can indirectly regulate the feeling, which is not." In other words, fake it until you get it, or jump in and then learn to swim!

My favorite story to illustrate this philosophy is about a great industrial fire at a plant down in a valley. Calls went out to the major fire companies to respond and put out the fire. Not one that responded could extinguish the fire. They couldn't even get close due to the intense heat. One by one they tried and failed. They all pretty much resigned themselves to the fact that it would be impossible to put that fire out. One local television station, however, broadcast an "APB" for any and all fire companies to respond. The fire company that could put out the fire would receive a ten-thousand-dollar reward. Many more fire companies showed up; however, the result was always the same–they failed. But just when all looked hopeless, over the crest of the mountain came one pickup truck, one driver, and two men in back with a bucket of water, a bucket of sand, and a blanket. The pickup came roaring down the valley and flew past all of the huge hook-and-ladder trucks from the big city. It drove right into the center of the huge inferno. Though the view was blurry, the onlookers could see the three men working frantically to put out the fire. Guess what—they did! They put out the fire that everyone else said could not be extinguished. The men were heroes. The television station wrote out the check to that small town fire company, and as they were going off the air, the TV reporter asked the driver one final question: "What are you going to do with the money?"

The driver, without blinking an eye, said, "The first thing I'm going to do is get the brakes on the truck fixed!"

As I said, until you believe, fake it. Just throw yourself into it, always with great enthusiasm and energy.

One of the best stories I've heard regarding "believing" comes from my outstanding long-time assistant coach and friend, Jack Holloway. Jack was not only a superb linebacker and offensive line coach, but was also the 2000 National High School Wrestling Coach of the Year—a fitting tribute to a great coach and motivator. Jack loves to tell a story he first heard from the late sportscaster Tom Mees of ESPN fame. Tom was a University of Delaware grad who got his broadcasting start doing Blue Hen football and basketball games. He later became one of the original anchors along with Chris Berman on "Sportscenter" during ESPN's inaugural year in 1979. Jack used this story often to motivate our players, his wrestlers and in his role as Athletic Director, all of our school's student-athletes and coaches. To this day, I never tire of hearing him tell this story in his own unique way.

The story recounts a time when the great high-wire aerialist, Karl Wallenda, was being interviewed by a reporter. Wallenda had just successfully completed a crossing of Niagara Falls on a high wire, pushing a wheelbarrow loaded with bricks. As he was preparing to cross back over to the other side, the reporter asked him if he was a "positive thinker." Wallenda replied, "No, I'm a positive believer." Seeing the confusion on the reporter's face, Wallenda asked him, "Do you think I can go back across the Falls?"

The reporter answered, "Yes, I think you can."

"Well that's positive thinking, not positive believing," Wallenda said.

Still confused, the reporter asked, "What's the difference?"

Wallenda answered, as he was removing the bricks from the wheelbarrow, "Hop in, I'll show you!"

The Wallenda story is a great one to illustrate the point to your players that belief must be a total commitment. It's like the chicken and the pig who were sitting down to breakfast. The pig said, "What are you having for breakfast?"

The chicken said, "Ham and eggs."

The pig said, "That's fine for you. For you that's only a contribution; for me, it's a total commitment!"

Do you want to win the big one? Be a pig! Be totally committed.

NEVER QUIT:
Don't Ever Give Up

Unless you're Knute Rockne, Vince Lombardi, Bud Wilkinson, Bear Bryant, Eddie Robinson, Bobby Bowden, Joe Paterno, or my home-state favorite Tubby Raymond, winning won't come easily. Not to say that these legendary coaches didn't have to struggle. But they worked hard, and they were truly gifted coaches. Most of us are not in their league. Some coaches may be blessed with great talent at their schools, but most do not have a consistent talent pool to draw from. So how can the average coach with average talent ever hope to win the big game? I have already said this several times: never quit!

Perseverance is the hallmark of success. You must learn to embrace defeat in order to obtain success. Does it sound crazy? Not really; just look at history. Anytime you get overwhelmed and feel like quitting, remember this historic giant as described by inspirational writer Larry Bielat in his book *Winning Words*:

He failed in business in '32.

He ran as a state legislator and lost in '32.

He tried business again and failed in '33.

His sweetheart died in '35.

He had a nervous breakdown in '36.

He ran for State Elector in '40 after he regained his health.

He was defeated for congress in '43, defeated again for congress in '48, defeated when he ran for Senate in '55 and defeated for vice president of the United States in '56.

He ran for the Senate again in '58 and lost.

This man never quit.

He kept trying til the last.

In 1860, this man, Abraham Lincoln, was elected President of the United States of America.

In our players' handbook I have always featured the famous picture of a stork trying to eat a frog. The frog has his hands around the stork's neck and is holding on for dear life. The message of the cartoon is unmistakable: never give up! Even when failure looks imminent, never quit. To further illustrate our determination never to quit, I would describe this scenario: "If you are standing on the one-yard line and someone is running for a touchdown ninety yards away, start running and don't stop until he crosses the goal line."

This approach may seem extreme, but it symbolized our desire never to quit despite the odds. Even if we were losing by a large margin, we still wanted to give everything we had right up to the final whistle. If you have a team that is willing to chase a runner at full speed from ninety yards away, you have a team that will never quit!

Sometimes being the last to quit is the only margin of victory. Your opponent may be equally as committed to winning as you are, but if you instill in your team that they will never quit until the final

DON'T EVER GIVE UP!

gun sounds, it may be the one thing that separates you from your opponent. As scientist Louis Pasteur once said, "Let me tell you the secret that has led me to my goal. My strength lies solely in my tenacity."

Zig Ziglar, in his book *Breaking through to the Next Level*, wrote about the difference between winning teams and losing teams. He cites a study done by the Big Ten Conference that reinforces the importance of never quitting. More accurately, it supports the fact that being the "last to quit" is a measurable factor in determining the victor from the vanquished. In this study, the difference between first and second place was the difference in the length of time in total effort. Game film analysis showed, "The difference between the team that finished first versus the team that finished last was nine-tenths of a second spent in all-out effort. The difference between first and second place was five-tenths of a second in total effort. . . . The average team went all-out two and seven-tenths seconds on every play." That's statistical proof that "not quitting" (or at least being the "last to quit") pays huge dividends.

Being the "last to quit" took on a unique dimension in a 1912 boxing match between Ad Wolgast and "Mexican Joe" Rivers. As reported in Steve Riach's *Amazing but True Sport Stories,* the record shows that on July 4, 1912, in Vernon, California, Wolgast and Rivers simultaneously knocked each other out in the thirteenth round of a hotly contested lightweight title fight. This double knockout was the only one ever recorded in title fight history. Both men were unconscious and sprawled out on the mat. The referee, Jack Walch, went over to Wolgast and propped him up against the ropes. He then went over to Rivers and counted him out. The crowd went crazy! No one settled down until Walch finally announced why he had awarded the fight to the champion Wolgast. He simply said, "He fell last."

This mindset is truly needed in order to be successful. Without it, the obstacles and hardships that every coach and team must face will too often prevail. With it, the losses and hardships become building blocks for future success for the team that never quits. Do you want to be successful? Take a page from "Pistol Pete" Maravich when he said, "Character never quits, and with patience and persistence, dreams do come true." (This is another quote from Riach's book.)

Dreams can come true, but sometimes persistence can take on bizarre proportions. For example, I think the movie *Tin Cup*, starring Kevin Costner, must have taken its theme from the real-life golf drama of Kelley Stroud. Stroud was playing in the 1960 Portland, Oregon, Amateur Golf Championship. His tee shot on the par 3, 148-yard sixteenth hole, found the water hazard in front of the green. His second and third shots also found the watery grave. Do the math. He was already laying six, but Kelley Stroud did not quit! He stubbornly proceeded to put down his fourth shot (or seventh, counting penalties) from the original tee box area. His final shot sailed straight as an arrow and found the bottom of the cup – a belated four-over-par "hole in one"?

Don't get me wrong; I wouldn't want this guy coaching my team, but I would want him playing for me. He is the type of player who will work and work and never quit until he gets it right!

Maybe the most memorable statement about never quitting was made by the late North Carolina State basketball coach Jim Valvano. Jim became an instant celebrity with his famous run on the court following the 1983 NCAA Basketball Championship game with the University of Houston. His Wolfpack team was a decided underdog in the battle with the likes of Houston's Hakeem Olajuwon and Clyde Drexler. The Wolfpack won a thriller at the end of regulation time with a dunk off a missed shot at the buzzer. The scoreboard read "North Carolina State: 54 – University of Houston: 52." I'll never forget the way Coach Valvano ran onto the court looking for someone to hug!

That memory pales in comparison to the speech that Jim Valvano gave at the 1993 ESPY awards show. Coach V was nearing the end of his valiant battle with bone cancer. He was speaking to the audience after receiving the first Arthur Ashe Courage and

Humanitarian Award. He was fighting for the biggest upset of his life—the cure for cancer. That evening he announced the creation of the V Foundation for cancer research. He dedicated the brief amount of time that he had left to the ongoing search for a cancer cure. He knew that it would be too late for him, but hopefully not for his children and others. He proclaimed the unforgettable motto for the V Foundation: "Don't give up. Don't ever give up."

That philosophy is at the heart of the "art of the upset." It won him and his team a national championship, but it also won him an ongoing legacy in the search for the cure for cancer. Coach V was triumphant in garnering tremendous attention and money for the cancer cause. Good friends Dick Vitale, Mike Krzyzewski, and a host of others still help carry on the dream of Jim Valvano and the V Foundation. Coach V summed it up best when he said, "I think you have an enthusiasm for life. You have a dream, a goal. You have to be willing to work for it." His dream to cure cancer did not come to be during his lifetime, but my bet is that because of his lasting influence, his dream will one day be a reality. It will be one of the greatest upsets of all!

NEVER QUIT:
Patience and Perseverance

The "never quit" mindset is the essential part of the upset equation. But there is another factor in the equation that cannot be overlooked – patience. For some, the upsets and program turnarounds may come quickly. Boise State and the University of South Florida, for example, are the fastest programs in college Division I football to go from program inception to ranking in the top twenty-five nationally. The meteoric success of these programs is phenomenal, but it is not the norm. For the rest of us the process may be more gradual. That is exactly how you must view it. It is a process. It takes time to put into place the mindset of the upset. The upset is a complete program by-product. Don't rush it. Work diligently to put into place all of the necessary ingredients, and it will evolve and happen.

Too many lose patience and quit long before the mindset changes have had time to materialize and take root. I was taught this (patience and persistence) as a small child. I'll bet you were too. Don't you remember the story of the tortoise and the hare? The race doesn't always go to the swifter runner. With this in mind, I think it would be good to adopt the motto of the U.S. Naval Construction

Battalions, better known as the "Seebees": "The difficult we do at once; the impossible takes a little longer." So stay at it and make persistence, determination, and patience your focus.

Former President Calvin Coolidge once said: "Nothing in the world can take the place of persistence. Talent will not; nothing is more common than unsuccessful men with talent. Genius will not; un-rewarded genius is almost a proverb. Education will not; the world is full of educated derelicts. Persistence and determination alone are omnipotent. The slogan 'press on' has solved and always will solve the problems of the human race." A modern version of this idea comes from William Bennett, former Secretary of Education and "Drug Czar" under presidents Reagan and Bush. Bennett said, "Much good that might have been achieved in the world is lost through hesitation, faltering, wavering, vacillating, or just not sticking to it . . . so whatever you are facing, just persevere!"

An Associated Press article published on July 5, 2008, illustrates quite well the relationship of perseverance to success. Christian Smith was listed as the thirty-first qualifier in the 800-meter race to determine who would represent the U.S. in the 2008 Olympics in Beijing, China. Smith dived and literally slid his way across the finish line to secure third place and the last spot on the Olympic team in this event. He had to dive to defeat a four-time national champion who was only inches ahead of him. When asked what lesson can be learned from his "upset" performance he replied, "I would say perseverance. It's essentially hammering away at it and keeping the focus and having my goals. Nobody expected me to be an Olympian." What made it even more remarkable was the fact that Christian Smith had to sit out the entire 2007 track season with a ruptured appendix and subsequent infection that created a huge abscess in his abdomen. He persevered, however, and never gave up on his dream.

Share these stories of perseverance and the "never quit" mindset with your players. The stories have had a profound effect on me. I love to read them and share them with others. They are truly inspirational. When these stories are shared with your team, you will be instilling within them the attitude of the upset. They can conquer great things despite overwhelming odds. They can rise above the expectations of others and even of themselves. Give them the vision of success and let their hard work, perseverance and "never quit" attitude define their efforts. Their patience and their efforts will be rewarded. They will truly reap the fruits of their labor.

THE PERFECT COMBO:
Never Quit and Hard Work

The Erik Jones Story

In *The Daily Motivator to Go*, Ralph Marston says, "You can accomplish anything, anything, when you consistently apply effort for as long as it takes." Following the same train of thought, I always wanted our teams to live by another famous quote from the legendary coach of the Green Bay Packers, Vince Lombardi. He said, "The harder you work, the harder it is to surrender."

Former Milwaukee Brewers' baseball manager Dave Bristol once put a comical twist to this concept of extra work and effort. His team was mired in a slump, and no relief was in sight. Bristol finally decided that extra work was the only solution to the team's poor play. He announced, "There'll be two buses leaving the hotel for the park tomorrow. The two o'clock bus will be for those who need a little extra work. The empty bus will leave at five o'clock!"

Knowing how to struggle and fight under any and all circumstances will provide your players with a blueprint for success in life. The older one gets, the more one realizes the value of hard work and never quitting. Historically, most successful people were not brilliantly gifted. The overwhelming majority did not have success handed to them on a silver platter. As Marcus Washling said, "Those at the top of the mountain didn't fall there!" Most had to work hard and long to achieve success. They were persistent. If Heinz had quit at 56 varieties, we wouldn't have "Heinz 57." We wouldn't have "Preparation H," either, if they had stopped at "G."

Those are lighthearted illustrations, but to throw a little more "light" on the subject, all you have to do is study the life of Thomas Edison to get a great feel for this and to drive home the point. After all, it took Edison almost 10,000 tries before he perfected his light bulb!

One of my former quarterbacks is a great example of the power of persistence coupled with hard work. Erik Jones was a slender young ninth-grade kid with big dreams. He imagined himself as the starting quarterback for our team. There was a problem; no one else had the same vision. (I have to admit, at that time, I never dreamed he would someday fulfill his dream and go even farther.) It all started in middle school. One of my best friends, Richard Farmer, was teaching and coaching at George Read Middle School. Richard was an outstanding teacher, coach, and later administrator in our district. He was and still is a master motivator. I think that if you looked up the combination word "positive enthusiasm" in the dictionary, you would find it spelled "Richard Farmer."

Erik was one of his middle-school players. Richard knew that Erik was struggling as a student and started to work with him to instill within him a desire to do better. That's where the story starts, but it did not stop there. Erik was basically our last-string quarterback as a freshman. Through hard work and determination, he progressed slowly up the ranks. His sophomore year, however, still had Erik at the back of the pack for prospective starting JV quarterbacks. By his junior year he had risen to second string JV, and by the end of the year he was sharing the starting JV quarterback duties.

We had a good crop of young men at quarterback that year, and there was healthy competition for the starting job. Erik came to me at the conclusion of his junior year and told me, "Coach, I'm going to be your starting quarterback next year!"

I said, "Fine, but you've got a lot of work to do." I can honestly say that I have seen very few individuals work harder to obtain a goal than Erik Jones. I loaned him a brand-new football to work out with in the off-season. Very soon, Erik was back asking me for another one. When I inquired about the first ball, he produced a severely worn-out ball with blown-out seams and worn-down laces. It resembled a rugby ball more than a football. I gave him a new ball. He brought that ball back in an even worse condition. The bladder was bubbling out between the seams. I gave him another new ball. This continued until the first day of practice in his senior year. What a transformation! The skinny kid was now a weight-trained and dedicated student-athlete who could throw a ball a country mile on target.

Erik not only started for us that year, but also earned First Team All-State and All-Conference honors at quarterback. To say that I was proud of his hard work and dedication is an understatement. Erik earned a scholarship to attend Delaware State University and became a four-year starter who broke all of their previous passing records. I think, however, I am most proud of his academic accomplishments. Erik is now a college graduate with a Masters degree in business. He is teaching and coaching back at our school and doing an exceptional job. His story will continue to be an inspiration for all of our kids who are willing to work hard, "never quit," and pay the price for success.

Erik's story should also be inspiring for all who work with young people. It took an interest from Richard Farmer to start this journey forward. That interest planted the seed for academic and athletic success. From that point on, administrators, teachers, and coaches continued to nourish that interest. When inspiration turned into dedication and hard work by Erik, the results were spectacular.

CAN'T PLAY?
You Can Still Make Your Mark!

The Carl Eaton Story

I'll never forget Carl Eaton. I mentioned him earlier in my discussion of the importance of staff that support the team. Carl is an outstanding example of "never quit" determination and tenacity. His story exemplifies the "art of the upset" to its fullest.

Carl was a starting guard and linebacker for our 1992 state championship team. In addition to his exceptional playing ability, he was one of our team co-captains. Unfortunately, he suffered a season-ending knee injury in pre-season. Carl never played a down that season. So how is it that Carl holds a premiere place in the collective memory of our staff and team? His contribution to the success of our team was unparalleled.

Our team that year struggled early in the season. We lost our first two games of the year. One of our losses was to regional powerhouse Salesianum High School. My close friend and former Delaware Coach of the Year, George Glenn, was Salesianum's outstanding head coach. Coach Glenn was a passionate coach, and his team reflected that fire. In my entire career, I don't remember any team that dominated us to the degree that Salesianum did in that game. Salesianum never had a third or a fourth down in the entire game. You read it right! No third down situations and no punts! Because we always took great pride in our defense, it was an embarrassment.

We found ourselves faced with two losses in a row, with no relief in sight. We had to take an unprecedented three straight safeties in the next three games to pull out narrow victories. We were only a matter of a few points away from 0 and 5. We were the reigning state champions, but many of our outstanding seniors had graduated. Our team that fall was relatively inexperienced.

The pressure was on. I have always preached to our players that what happens to you is not as important as how you react to it. How you deal with what life throws at you is critical. I definitely subscribe to Charles Swindoll's statement on attitude:

"The longer I live, the more I realize the impact of attitude on life. Attitude to me is more important than facts. It is more important than the past, than education, than money, than circumstances, than failures, than successes, than what other people think or say or do. It is more important than appearance, giftedness or skill. It will make or break a company . . . a church . . . a home. The remarkable thing is we have a choice every day regarding the attitude we will embrace for that day. We cannot change our past . . . we cannot change the inevitable. The only thing we can do is play on the one string we have and that is our attitude . . . I am convinced that life is 10% what happens to me and 90% how I react to it. And so it is with you . . . We are in charge of our attitudes."

The staff did not feel that the team had "bought in" to our program totally. We didn't feel that they truly believed that if they followed our blueprint they would be successful. That's where Carl took over. He did not do it alone, but he was the key. Carl's reaction to his pre-season injury was remarkable. He accepted that he could not "change the inevitable." He was extremely frustrated; however, his commitment to the team was paramount. He and I talked many times about his role as a team leader who could not physically lead on the playing field. He became an unofficial coach, and his enthusiasm was infectious.

The other players observed how he handled his disappointment. They also absorbed his attitude of "I'll do whatever it takes to contribute to the success of this team." He pushed, encouraged, cajoled, and counseled the other players. He was a player, a coach, a cheerleader, and a source of inspiration to all of us. The team started to "jell" under his leadership. They "bought in" because he led by example and showed them what it meant to "buy into" the program.

We went on an eight-game winning streak that propelled us to a conference championship and enabled us to get a berth in the state championship tournament. We won the semi-final game and headed into the state championship game against our old foe Salesianum. Many outside the team felt that we could not win this game. I didn't blame them. They had seen our first game against Salesianum! Our team, however, didn't believe they couldn't win. Carl and the other seniors would not allow that thought.

We won, of course! We put on one of the greatest exhibitions of football that I have ever experienced. We won the game 21-0. We had a drive of twenty-one plays that ate up almost the entire third quarter. Wind gusts of thirty to forty miles an hour drove the wind-chill factor below zero. It was nearly impossible to throw, so it had to be done the old fashioned way—with purely physical football. It took courage to go toe-to-toe with Salesianum, and we knew they would never quit. But on our sideline were Carl and a group of players and coaches that believed in one another. It was a great upset against an outstanding opponent.

I have only given out one game ball after a game in my entire career (and we won seven state championships). That day, I gave the ball to Carl Eaton. He deserved it. He showed what unselfish commitment to a program means. He didn't just talk it; he lived it. He demonstrated to every player on that team that no matter what your role, you can contribute greatly to the success of your team.

Carl's story has been told to every young man who followed after him in our program. The message is clear: "Don't give up when you encounter a setback. Find your niche and contribute. You do make a difference. You do not have to start on offense or defense to be a contributor to the program. Put everything you have into the process and you will be rewarded." I've never seen a better example of "never quit" than the story of Carl Eaton.

By the way, after college, Carl returned to our team as a certified trainer and a coach. He wanted to give back and contribute to our program. Carl continued with the team after my retirement from coaching and found that under our new head coach (former player and assistant coach Bill C. Cole) the program is still the same – developing young boys into responsible young men. Carl is currently an assistant trainer with the Indiana Pacers professional basketball team.

LEADERSHIP
Declare Your Vision, Show Uncommon Commitment, and Expect Positive Results

Strong leadership is essential in developing a team that can master the "art of the upset." Outstanding leaders display similar skills, whether they are coaching a football team or managing a business. A recent article in the *JAS Coaching and Training Newsletter*, written by Air Force Reserve Major General William A. Cohen, outlines "Eight Keys to Leadership Greatness," which are particularly applicable to coaching. One of the most important keys is "Declare your vision." If you don't tell people in plain words what you hope to accomplish, how will they be able to help you attain it?

Harry S. Truman once said, "A great leader is a man who has the ability to get other people to do what they don't want to do and like it." Hard, disciplined practice and preparation for the upset is difficult. The best way to make your team "like it," is to get them to visualize the final outcome. You must communicate your vision to them. One year, I went so far as to have my players practice throwing their helmets up into the air in celebration of the upcoming win. It was done in fun; however, they got the point. To gain the upset, you must first visualize it. The team did the work; it was hard, but they bought in to the mindset of the upset. We made it fun and they "liked it."

One of my outstanding assistant coaches, Steve Lepre, likes to tell how I persuaded him to become a line coach. Our offensive tackle and defensive line coach, Howdy Duncan, had just retired. Howdy was a one-of-a-kind individual. The kids loved him, and so did the entire staff. He got the maximum out of each boy he ever coached. His retirement was a great blow to our tightly knit staff. Howdy's departure left big shoes to fill. Steve had been a stellar quarterback and defensive back in high school. He had never coached a down lineman in his life. But Steve is a gifted teacher and coach who has the ability to relate well with kids. He uses his great sense of humor combined with the ability to be tough when he has to be to get the job done. So, despite his inexperience, I knew that Steve would be the perfect fit.

He still jokes about the "pitch" I used to talk him into assuming this new role as line coach. I assured him that it would be a great boost to his young coaching career. By taking this assignment, he would vastly expand his knowledge of the game. He says that I already had decided that he would coach the line, but I made it appear that it was his choice. He is right! I asked him to make a difficult transition. Steve never blinked an eye and readily agreed to make the switch. That is Steve, always willing to do what is needed for the team. He not only made the transition, but he "liked it." He has since developed into a superb line coach.

"Show uncommon commitment" is another of the eight keys that I fully endorse. If you don't show your players that you are committed to the program in its entirety, they certainly won't be committed either. In my earlier years I lifted weights right along with the athletes in our conditioning program. I felt that they needed to see me working as well. No player will ever comprehend all the time and energy that coaches put into the program, so whenever an opportunity arises to demonstrate your commitment and dedication, seize it.

Another essential key is critical: "Expect positive results." You must believe that all the hard work and sacrifice will pay off. You must believe in your game plan, and you must believe in each other.

You can even take the negatives and turn them into a positive motivation. In the early 1900s, Andrew Carnegie commissioned the writer Napoleon Hill to research success. Hill identified a common thread shared by successful people and organizations: "Hidden within every disadvantage or obstacle lay an equally powerful opportunity. Successful leaders look for those opportunities." My coaches were actually happy when a mistake was made in our early pre-season scrimmages. For example, we wanted our defensive backs to get beat deep. What a great teaching tool! We would show our players the error in their technique and then drill them to perfection in the proper and correct way to defend. You have to follow up on this, however. You have to polish the skill or technique every day. As the old sea captain said about the brass instruments on the deck of his ship: "You have to polish them every day or they start to tarnish."

The last key that I want to highlight is "Take care of your people." Identify the wants and desires of your players (all of your players). The player lining up on the demo side of the ball is critical to the success of your team. Your starters will only be as good as the teammates who push them in practice. You have to provide them with incentives, however, and that means playing time, too. We initiated a "tee shirt and playing time award" for our non-starters. Whichever non-starter provided us with the best effort throughout the week was given a player-of-the-week tee shirt. This award also garnered playing time for him in the next game and an honorary co-captain's position at the pre-game coin toss. If we could, we started this player for at least the first series; he would always see substantial playing time if only on special teams.

I have already mentioned the axiom on leadership from Duke's Mike Krzyzewski. He says that the players must first believe in you; then and only then will they follow you. Respect and trust can't be bought. They must be earned. You can't preach one thing and then do another. If you do, you will be viewed by your players as untrustworthy.

In his book *A Scandalous Freedom,* Steve Brown tells a story about Abe Lincoln that illustrates this point. Prior to becoming President, Abe Lincoln attended a slave auction. He noticed a young African-American girl who was being offered to the highest bidder. Lincoln bid and won. After the purchase he talked with the girl and told her that she was now free.

She said, "Yeah. What does that mean?"

"It means that you are free" Lincoln replied.

"Does that mean I can say whatever I want to say?"

"Yes, it means you can say whatever you want to say."

Incredulously she asked, "Does it mean I can be whatever I want to be?"

"Yes, it means you are free and can go wherever you want to go."

"Then," said the young girl, "I think I'll go with you."

She was free to go anywhere she pleased, but she chose to follow Lincoln because she believed in him.

Leadership is about example. You can tell people anything you want. You can make rules and maxims and dole out rewards and punishments. But to really get someone to follow and to "buy in" to you and your program, you have to "walk the talk."

TEAM HANDBOOK

As I have said several times before, to get your team to buy in to your program, you have to define exactly what your program is. Every day, you have to preach to your team the core values and the philosophy of your program. You have to spell out exactly what makes your program unique and special. One tool we used for this purpose was our player handbook. It was not a playbook. It was a "blueprint" for success achieved by applying the mindset and attitude that we tried to instill in our players. I have taken a few pages out of the handbook to illustrate the reinforcement of the building blocks of our program that we worked on each and every day of the year.

The first page of the handbook was an open letter to the team:

In order to be successful in any endeavor, one has to dedicate himself. The dedication it takes to be successful in football is known by all who play the game. What separates the successful from the unsuccessful teams is the application of their dedication. There is a blueprint for success, which, if followed, will produce tremendous gains. Our blueprint is very simple:

1. Be responsible, strive for perfect attendance in school and at practice.
2. Study – your grades are important now and for the future. You must also study your football assignments and know them perfectly.
3. Surround yourself with positive people who share the same goals as you do. For example: good attendance, good grades, good behavior, good study and work skills.
4. Eat properly (good nutrition is a must for the totally conditioned athlete).
5. Stretch properly (injury prevention is a must).
6. Lift in our off-season and in-season weights and conditioning programs.
7. Work on your speed development and quickness drills (dot drill, plyometrics).
8. Practice your football skills.
9. Plan your work, then work your plan.
10. Memorize this saying (only 10 two-letter words): "If It Is To Be, It Is Up To Me."
11. When we start playing our games we will change the saying to the following: "If It Is To Be, It Is Up To Us."
12. Think "Team" and Dare to Dream!!!

We concluded the handbook with this final thought for the team:

If you are confused about any of our team rules or regulations, do the following:

Act in a manner which typifies our highest ideals. Ask yourself if your actions will affect others on our team. Remind yourself that the people in our school and the community hold us up to their children as an outstanding example–don't let them down. Remember that the goal of our football program is not just to win games, but also to help build character, poise, and pride in oneself, the team, the school and our community. Make your family proud of your actions. Make yourself proud to be a part of our program and our great tradition.

Good Luck, Coach Reynolds and Staff

SPORTSMANSHIP

I read an article by David C. McCasland about a football team from Nebraska, the Boys Town High School Cowboys. Their coach, Kevin Kush, views the game and the values that should be taught in their proper perspective. Every coach should take a page out of Kevin Kush's book. According to Coach Kush, "Victories at Boys Town are not won on a present day athletic field. They are won years from now in cities and towns across this country when our players become productive citizens." The article goes on to say, "His team plays to win while pursuing higher goals of sportsmanship, discipline and teamwork."

Coach Kush's Boys Town team was comprised of young men from diverse and challenging backgrounds. Abuse and neglect were common denominators for the entire team. Despite this, in 2005 the Cowboys achieved a stellar ten-win season, losing only in the semi-finals of the Nebraska High School Football Championships.

You can teach and coach values and win, and you can do it anywhere and with anyone willing to listen to you and your philosophy. It takes courage, character and patience, but look at the rewards: young men of value with values—values that will be passed on to their children and to all with whom they come into contact. What is it all about anyway? We all want to win, but never lose sight of the ultimate goal: to teach and mold young men. Tyrone Willingham, while coaching at Notre Dame, said it well: "When I started to develop a fondness, or my love for athletics, it was because athletics was a powerful way to influence youngsters to be better people. . . . The ultimate goal of athletics should be to help mold young people to be our leaders."

One of the best things that the State of Delaware has done was to institute a state championship category for sportsmanship. Each year, the Delaware Interscholastic Athletic Association awards a state championship banner to the school that has exhibited the highest form of sportsmanship for the entire school year. It is a coveted award. My school, William Penn, has had the honor of winning or sharing this award every year since its inception in 1998. Of all the state championship banners that hang on the walls of our gym, the Sportsmanship banner is the one that we are most proud of and hold in the highest regard.

DO IT THE RIGHT WAY

Whatever you do, never compromise your principles. Over the years, I have observed too many coaches who have done so. Fortunately, I have also observed many who have not; and I might add, have done so with spectacular results. One of my favorite stories involves one of my dear friends and long-time assistant coach, David Taylor. Dave was also our head baseball coach at the time. Dave was faced with a situation that involved two of his star baseball players. They had violated specific team rules. It would have been easy to compromise the rules. No one would have said anything. However, Dave understood the importance of the team concept: you can never treat the star player differently than you treat the last man on your team. If you succumb to that temptation, you will lose the confidence and respect of your players. But, what if your suspension of those players comes on the eve of the big game? Will you have the fortitude to hold your ground and stand by your principles, even if it means you jeopardize winning the game? Dave did! Not only did the team rally around him, but that team went on a winning streak that took them all the way to the state championship that year. The championship was won, principles were intact, invaluable lessons were learned by the younger players on the team, and a profound respect was forever gained by that coach and that team. The year was 1977, and we still talk about that team, that coach, and that championship season – not *because* they won, but *how* they won.

I can honestly say that in thirty years of coaching, twenty-seven as the head coach, we never asked a teacher to change a grade or give special consideration to a player. This is not a boast because it should be the norm – nothing special. Unfortunately, it isn't always that way with some coaches. My staff and I have talked to teachers about how we can help players achieve in their classes, but never with the goal of getting special treatment for them. As a matter of fact, many teachers came to us to help them motivate a particular player in their class. It was more of a reciprocal relationship aimed at helping the student-athlete achieve in all of his school endeavors.

You must run your program so that it is explicitly clear that your players are to be treated – and when necessary, punished–the same as all students in your school. When this is established, you not only run a clean program, but you gain the respect and support of your colleagues and the rest of the student body.

Sometimes it is a small thing that starts the erosion of student body and faculty support. For example, how about butting in line in the cafeteria? I ate all of my lunches in the cafeteria. As a teacher, I had the privilege of going to the front of the line. It was just one of the perks of being a teacher. I never used that privilege. My staff and I always preached to our players that if we ever caught them trying to butt in line there would be severe consequences. One football player butting in line starts the "talk." The "talk" usually begins with the statement, "They think they are better than the rest of us." That's all it takes to start a general dislike for the football "jocks" at your school.

To help set the tone, I always got at the end of the cafeteria line with the students and waited my turn. My hope was that the students and my players would see me doing this and know that we practiced what we preached.

To some it may seem like a trivial thing, but rest assured, it is not. Too many schools have double standards. If the goal is just to win, then it sometimes works in the short term, but it will always come back to haunt you over the long haul of your season or your career. Your players may win, but their success will not be respected. This advice may not seem to be germane to the topic, but nothing could be further from the truth. It is one of the building blocks that make it possible for you to consistently win the games you should win, and to win many of those games that no one except you, your staff, and your players thinks you can win. It's all about doing the right thing. It is the only way to run your program. You will teach more than football to your team when they see you abiding by the rules.

I heard Coach Lou Holtz at a clinic say the following: "The answers to these questions will determine your success or failure: 1. Can people trust me to do what's right? 2. Am I committed to doing my best? 3. Do I care about other people and show it? If the answers to these questions are 'Yes,' there is no way you can fail." An affirmative answer to the question, "Can people trust me to do what's right?" should become a cornerstone of your program's philosophy.

Focusing on doing things the right way will also help you keep football in perspective for your players and for yourself. The old adage that "nice guys finish last" is invalid. Just look at an article about the 2007 Smith Center Redmen High School football team in Kansas. On November 9, 2007, Joe Drape of the New York *Times* wrote about this remarkable team and the town of 1,931 people that loved them. At the time, Smith Center High had won fifty-one games in a row and three consecutive state championships. They had also outscored their opponents 704-0. When asked to comment on their success, head coach Roger Barta had this to say: "What we do around here real well is raise kids. None of this is really about football. We're going to get scored on eventually and lose a game, and that doesn't mean anything. What I hope we're doing is sending kids into life who know that every day means something."

Coach Barta's philosophy fits well with a great quote from Albert Einstein: "Try not to become a man of success, but rather to become a man of value." For me that's proof that doing things the right way is a winning way, and it should be the only way. Coach Barta is living proof that nice guys do finish first!

ACADEMICS

Your players can't play if they aren't eligible! We took this to heart, and during my career I lost a few excellent players because of poor grades when we needed them most. Our report cards always came out right before the state tournament at the end of the season. We tried to avoid this type of loss at all costs. We instituted a study hall for our players and required all players who were on academic watch to attend study hall before practice each day. Our school's National Honor Society students served as tutors. Each student-athlete had to stay for a minimum of thirty to forty minutes before reporting to the practice field.

We structured practice so that the study hall impacted us as little as possible. We did our pre-practice routine and form tackling drills followed by our kicking game. We then did our group and team defense followed by our group and team offense. This structure served us well, and it definitely cut down on the number of failures at the end of the season.

Our emphasis on schoolwork was also our way of showing our players that they were students first and athletes second. We used grade sheets to track the academic progress of our players. Our faculty was very supportive; each subject teacher would evaluate the student's progress by the use of a simple check-off system. The main things we wanted to know were whether or not they were going to class, doing their homework, passing their tests, and behaving in class. We also followed up in the off-season with our students who were performing marginally. Jack Carney, who was our academic football counselor, and I would put together a list of the "at risk" students and meet with them to review their academic goals. This constant monitoring was necessary to make sure that they knew that their progress was important to us all year long, not just during football season.

We also guided our players through the college selection and recruitment process. Jack and I produced a college-recruiting brochure in which we outlined the NCAA's SAT requirements and offered a host of helpful hints on how to evaluate schools. Our players' parents appreciated this. Many of our parents had no experience with the college entrance process and the financial aid forms that seem like Greek to the uninitiated.

Coach Bill C. Cole, who succeeded me as head coach, has done a particularly good job in this area. Through their efforts, Bill and his staff have drastically reduced the number of players lost due to ineligibility. In one recent year they didn't lose a single player to poor grades. When you consider that our district has very challenging academic standards, that accomplishment serves as testimony to the dedication and hard work of Bill and his staff. Bill is teaching his players the "right things." He definitely keeps football in perspective.

Your players' academic achievement must remain your main objective. After that, you can work like crazy to help your players be the best football players that they can be. What a great combination – a true student-athlete.

One last note on this subject: I found that some players were not carrying notebooks and other necessary "academic equipment" with them during the school day. Sadly, many of their peers made fun of those who took academics seriously. I took a note from Joe Paterno on this one and told them that I wanted only "nerds" on our team. We laid down the law and told them that they would be doing extra-curricular conditioning drills if they were caught without their note-books, pens, pencils, etc. I tried to give them an easy out with their unmotivated peers. They were instructed to tell them that it was a team rule; if they wanted to play they had to carry the books and do the work. From what I observed, most of their critics understood why they would comply and not want to run extra sprints. Whatever you have to do to remove the stigma from being a serious student, you have to do. You owe it to your players; their futures depend on it.

WRITTEN TEAM PHILOSOPHY

We have a written team philosophy of brotherhood. Our brotherhood verse was written by Neale Clopper, long-time guidance counselor at William Penn High School. Neale's son Mike was a starting halfback on our team at the time that he wrote it. I also have to add that Neale was a personal friend and a great motivator in the weight room. Neale joined me in running our off-season weightlifting program and later ran the program, both in-season and off-season, He mastered Dr. Greg Shepard's "Bigger, Faster, Stronger" program and instructed our players in its use. Neale became an exceptional weightlifter in his own right and worked right along with our players. In other words, he practiced what he preached and provided inspiration for all of us.

Our team name was the Colonials, and the main theme of the verse was that we were a "Colonial Football Brotherhood." We didn't care what race or color you were because the only colors we saw were our team colors, cherry and black. A summary just won't do it justice, so I have included the brotherhood verse in its entirety:

The Colonial Football Brotherhood

We are the William Penn Colonial's football team.

We are not white players or black players.

We are "Cherry and Black" players.

There is no race; there are only Colonials.

There is no me; there is only we,

For we are a brotherhood.

Our goals are to win and be champions, but if fate decrees we cannot be champions,

We will work to have the attitude of champions.

In practice and games we will strive for total dedication, total intensity, total enthusiasm,

Every player, every play; for the score is not as important as the effort.

As a team we will work to become closer.

When a brother is down, we will pick him up.

We will be happy in the successes of our brothers,

For jealousy has no place on our team.

We will not criticize each other; we will help each other.

Adversity will not drive us apart; it will bring us together.

For football careers will too soon be over – but the friendships we form will last forever.

As we walk the halls of William Penn we will adhere to the ideals of the brotherhood.

Because we know if we achieve our goals on the field,

We will be better people off the field.

For the ideals of dedication, loyalty, sportsmanship,

Enthusiasm, honesty, and intensity in the game of football

Are goals that are transferable in life.

And if we can achieve them we will leave William Penn as men.
Because maturity is not an age but an attitude – the
Attitude of the Colonial Brotherhood.

I think Neale's "Colonial Football Brotherhood" verse fits perfectly with our team song. Our team song reads "For every single one of us, we'll all stick up for the rest of us," and the "Brotherhood" verse reinforces this with, "When a brother is down we will pick him up." I wanted my teams to reflect this spirit of unity in everything that we did. We felt that the brotherhood verse and our team song were constant reminders of our team philosophy.

With our team verse and song, I hoped to emulate one of the best examples of brotherhood that I have ever encountered. According to a report widely circulated on the Internet, at a Special Olympics competition in Seattle, Washington, a group of nine physically and mentally challenged athletes prepared to run the 100-yard dash. When the gun sounded, eight of the nine runners joyously took off from the starting line. One small boy, however, stumbled and fell on the asphalt and began to cry. The others heard the cry and immediately slowed down and looked back at their fallen buddy. Every single one of them went back to console him. One girl with Down syndrome bent down, gave him a kiss, and said, "This will make it better." They picked up the little boy and all nine walked to the finish line with arms linked together. The audience roared approval, and to this day I'm sure that no one there will ever forget that scene and those athletes. They were winners, each and every one of them. It was a win for sportsmanship and brotherhood: "For every single one of us, we all stick up for the rest of us."

Do you want the upset? Then do it right. Tell your team these stories and watch them win now on the field and later, in life.

GREAT UPSETS

One year we were trying to gear up for a particularly big game. We were a decided underdog in this contest. Assistant coach Jack Holloway gave me an idea that he used with his wrestling team. We had our team gather all of the articles on great upsets that they could find. It was a homework assignment, but a fun one! The players and coaches gathered the articles and pictures and then shared them with the rest of the team. It was a great way to infuse positive outcome thoughts into our preparation for the upcoming big game. We immersed ourselves in stories of underdogs who overcame great odds to win. Several of the illustrations that follow came from that assignment. Try it, it works!

Stories of upsets from other sports can be effective in motivating your team. For example, how do you suppose Buster Douglas felt when he beat Mike Tyson? The odds-makers had the fight off the charts. No way could it be done. Read the accounts – it happened!

How did you feel when you watched the 2000 Olympic Greco-Roman wrestling match between Siberian born Aleksandr Karelin, the "Russian Bear," and Rulon Gardner of the United States? To look at them physically and compare their records, it would be an act of futility to hope that Rulon would even have a ghost of a chance to beat Karelin. In 1988, Karelin defeated four straight opponents to earn his way into the Olympic championship match. With 30 seconds to go he was trailing Bulgaria's Rangel Gerovski 3-0. Karelin used a reverse body lift, worth five points, to win the first of three straight Olympic gold medals. This "Gentle Giant," as some called him, went on a thirteen-year undefeated streak. While winning the gold in 1992, only one of Karelin's opponents held out for the entire time limit. In 1996, he was able to outscore all five of his opponents 25-0, becoming the first Olympic wrestler to win the same weight division three times.

To render any other opinion than to conclude that the Russian Bear would win the 2000 Olympic Gold Medal would have been folly. That is not what happened, however. Karelin suffered what some feel was a rare loss of focus, enabling Rulon Gardner to hold on to win the match 1-0 and the coveted gold medal, as well. He also won the hearts and minds of sports lovers everywhere.

This upset was a truly exciting and inspirational moment in Olympic history. Rulon won because he believed he could win. No one, I mean no one, would have agreed with him before the match. But Rulon is another example of what it takes to make the elusive upset a reality. It takes belief, perspiration, inspiration, and a "never quit" attitude. He combined all of those elements, and the 2000 Greco-Roman wrestling gold medal adorns his neck, a visible symbol of the "art of the upset."

Rulon was not finished with stunning upsets, however. In 2002, he lost a toe to frostbite when he became stranded while snowmobiling in Wyoming. He survived a motorcycle accident in 2004 after being struck by an automobile. In 2004, he also claimed the Olympic bronze medal and symbolically announced his retirement by leaving his shoes on the mat.

Rulon's story is not complete without one more tale of his odds-defying life. In February of 2007, he and two friends were flying low in a small engine plane that struck water. All three of the men were able to get out of the plane before it sank, but they had to swim for over an hour in 44-degree water. When they finally reached shore, they had to spend the night without any shelter. They were rescued a day later. One ranger at the park area where they crashed said, "It takes only about 30 minutes for someone swimming in 44-degree water to start suffering the effects of hypothermia, so the fact that they swam in it for an hour, not to mention surviving the plane crash and the night without fire or shelter, is pretty amazing." It is not so amazing to me when you consider whom we're talking about. Rulon never worried about the odds. He only knew that you never, never quit! Rulon Gardner epitomizes the word "upset" both in sport and in life.

Nothing compares, however, to the defeat of the seemingly invincible Russian ice hockey team by the U. S. team at the Lake Placid Olympics in 1980. The news of that win reverberated through-out America and the world like a sonic boom. Had the U.S. team read and believed the papers the preceding week, they wouldn't have bothered to show up. The United States team was seeded seventh out of twelve teams—not even in the upper half of the seeded teams. The U.S. team was also coming off a very poor showing one week earlier in an exhibition game with the Soviet juggernaut. They lost that one to the Soviets, 10-3, but then came the Olympic Games.

Achieving a 4-0-1 record, the U.S. team fought their way into position for a semi-final showdown with the Russians. Playing in front of a frenzied American audience, the U.S. team clawed their way to a 4-3 win. Goalie Jim Craig made a remarkable 39 saves in the game, with team captain Mike Eruzione scoring the game-winning goal in the third period.

Anticlimactically, the United States went on to defeat Finland, 4-2, to win the gold. Long-time ABC television announcer Al Michaels, now of *Monday Night Football* fame, asked the obvious question as the final seconds ticked away: "Do you believe in miracles?" It wasn't a miracle; it was an "upset," one that had been cultivated in the minds and hearts of a great team whose players chose to believe in each other rather than the critics. The win is a testament to their mindset for the upset. They were focused and locked into their belief in each other and their mission. They refused to lose. It's amazing what can be done when you take a bunch of guys who don't care who gets the credit as long as the job gets done.

There is one more Olympic example that helps tell the story of overcoming great odds and winning. It is the story of the U. S. "Magnificent Seven" women's gymnastic team at the 1996 Olympic Games in Atlanta, Georgia. Seven young American girls vaulted their way into the record books and Olympic lore. The super-talented Russian team anticipated an easy run for the gold. At least that's what the sports writers covering the Games thought. Little did they know that "upset" was in the air.

First place and a gold medal were riding on the final apparatus competition, the vault. Amanda Borden, Amy Chow, Dominique Dawes, Shannon Miller, Dominique Moceanu, Jacie Phelps, and little-known Kerri Strug were pulling out all the stops so that the United States could win its first-ever gold in women's gymnastics. Dominique Moceanu, who had just recovered from a leg stress fracture prior to the Olympics, slipped on both of her vaults. The U.S. team and everyone else in the world knew that it would be up to the last competitor, Kerri Strug. On her first vault, Kerri slipped on her landing and injured her leg. Coach Bela Karoli encouraged her and asked if she could continue to compete. Kerri said she could go on. Despite obvious pain, she vaulted her way into history. Her coach carried her off the mat basking in the approbation of the team, her nation and the world. The upset was secured; the United States had won the gold!

Again, the upset and her performance were not miracles. The victory was the culmination of a long process that had started back in Tucson, Arizona, where at age 13, Kerri started to work with Bela Karoli six to seven days a week, eight hours a day. The seed of the upset was planted when Kerri tore a stomach muscle that sidelined her from training and competing for six months. It continued to be cultivated when a back injury sidelined her for another six months. She always persevered, she never gave up, and she never quit. Kerri Strug and the other gymnasts of the "Magnificent Seven" earned their place in Olympic history and in my own personal "Hall of Upsets."

MORE UPSETS

C*inderella Man*, a film released in 2005, chronicles the rags-to-riches story of boxer James Braddock (played by Russell Crowe). Turning pro in 1926, Braddock worked his way up the ladder in the turbulent fight world of New York City. In 1929, he fought light heavyweight Jimmy Slattery for the title. Braddock lost a close gut-wrenching 15-round decision. That fight and the ensuing stock market crash sent Braddock into a financial and emotional tailspin, but he never gave up hope. He worked hard on what jobs he could find and even harder in the gym. It was perseverance that won a long 5-year battle back. In 1934, Braddock had upset wins over Corn Griffin and John Henry Lewis.

Finally, on June 13, 1935, he got the chance of a lifetime. He got a title shot with heavyweight champion Max Baer. Braddock was a ten-to-one underdog, but the blueprint for the upset was in place: perseverance, determination, focus, hard work, and "hunger." He was hungry to achieve a goal that he had set and pursued with a passion. Braddock defeated Baer that day in what was described in the papers as the "greatest fistic upset since the defeat of John L. Sullivan by Jim Corbett." That one defining moment sent James J. Braddock to the

International Boxing Hall of Fame in 2001. Braddock's formula for success echoes a sentiment earlier stated by scientist Louis Pasteur: "Let me tell you the secret that has led to my goal. My strength lies solely in my tenacity." Setting a goal and staying the course despite setbacks can make success a reality.

If you follow collegiate basketball's March Madness at all, you know some other "Cinderella" upset stories. Small schools like Weber State, Coppin State, Gonzaga, Hampton and Valparaiso, to name a few, have had huge upset wins in recent years. It seems that without exception every year promises another big victory by an unheralded school. It happens in every sport. The ESPY Awards, created by ESPN in 1993 to honor "Excellence in Sports Performance Yearly," recognize this phenomenon. In 2004, ESPN added a category for "Upsets." The 2005 ESPY Upset award went to Bucknell for its upset of third-ranked Kansas in basketball. Bucknell was playing in its first NCAA Tournament since 1989 vs. a Kansas program that had participated in 107 tourney contests. Kansas currently ranks fourth in all-time tourney appearances. This particular Kansas senior class had competed in two Final Fours.

Bucknell was not alone in the fan-polled voting for best upset of the year. Vermont's victory over Syracuse and Puerto Rico's win over the 2004 U.S. "Dream Team" in Athens, Greece, also made the list. Even a horse, Giacomo, got into the act. Giacomo won the Kentucky Derby as a 50-1 underdog. Venus Williams won Wimbledon in 2007 as the highest seed ever to win. She was ranked thirty-first at the time. And how about Boise State vs. Oklahoma in the 2007 Fiesta Bowl game? That was one great upset! Some long-time observers of the sport say that it was possibly the greatest bowl game of all time.

In choosing the greatest college upsets there will always be debate. But a 2007 online poll did a pretty good job of coming up with four that should always be on everyone's top-ten list. The poll rated the Appalachian State Mountaineers' upset win over fifth-ranked Michigan in front of 110,000 enthusiastic Wolverine fans as the top one. Michigan had just put on an unbelievable push to take the lead late in the fourth quarter. Refusing to lose, the Mountaineers were able to drive sixty-nine yards with no timeouts remaining and score the go-ahead field goal in just one minute and eleven seconds—but it wasn't over. Michigan proceeded to move the ball down to the twenty-yard line with just six seconds left on the clock and the chance to win the game with a thirty-seven yard field goal. The ball was snapped, placed down, kicked, and blocked! The shock took a few seconds to sink in and the "thrill of victory and the agony of defeat" were visited once again. No Division I-AA team had ever beaten an Associated Press ranked team since the 1978 Division I subdivisions were created.

There is more to this story than the 34-32 upset victory for Appalachian State. It involves the way the losing coach, Lloyd Carr, handled the defeat. He did it with tremendous class. You can imagine the disappointment and the resultant criticism that he had to endure. But a day after the defeat, he called Coach Jerry Moore and told him how impressed he was with him and his team's accomplishment. Jerry Moore later revealed in an interview that he wished that he had tape-recorded the call. He marveled at the sportsmanship and class that was demonstrated by Coach Carr. Carr's phone call was also an example of an "upset." It was a win over the norm. Too many coaches and players would point fingers, make excuses, and try to distance themselves from such a staggering loss – not Lloyd Carr. He handled it with the class of a champion.

The poll went on to identify three other great upsets. Voters ranked the number two greatest upset as the Boise State win over

Oklahoma in the 2007 Fiesta Bowl. I know I will never forget the fourth-down hook and lateral touchdown play with only seven seconds left on the clock. That was followed by an equally incredible two-point conversion play that fooled everyone on and off the field. Trailing by one point, Boise State faked a pass right and handed back to a fleet Ian Johnson, who raced into the end zone for the 43-42 point win.

Number three on the list was the 1982 Chaminade basketball victory over first-ranked Virginia. Many claim this one to be the biggest upset in college basketball history. It was followed by the number four-rated upset that saw the George Mason Patriots beat the number one-seeded Connecticut basketball team in the 2005 NCAA Tournament. That win propelled George Mason into the Final Four as an eleven seed. Whether you agree with these rankings or not, they are all memorable and remarkable upsets.

No one is immune from or incapable of obtaining the coveted upset. Look at what occurred on "Upset Weekend" (September 28 and 29, 2007). Nine of the top twenty-five ranked Bowl Subdivision teams lost! Of the top-ranked teams, numbers 3, 4, 5, 7, 10, 11, 13, 21, and 22 were upset. Only the number eleven-ranked University of Oregon's loss to number six-ranked California cannot be classified as an upset. Even the number one- and number nine-ranked teams only won by a margin of three points. The very next week the number two- and number five-ranked teams were upset. One of those, the 2007 University of Southern California vs. Stanford game, was a classic. Southern Cal was 4-0, and ranked number two in the country. Stanford was 1-3 and unranked. Stanford was a pre-game 41-point underdog, having been outscored 141-51 in their previous three PAC-10 games. Someone forgot to tell Stanford that they didn't have a prayer of a chance to win the game. The final score was a remarkable

24-23 upset win for Stanford. That week of upsets was followed by the number one and number two teams in the nation losing the very next Saturday.

I cannot recall a three-week period of time that produced so many upsets of the top teams in the nation. I was so intrigued that I conducted a study of all college football upsets that occurred during the 2007 season. I think 2007 should be called the "Season of the Upset." Just look at the statistics I compiled based on an analysis of four major polls: AP, BCS, Harris Interactive, and the Coaches' poll. When I started to break the season down into meaningful "upset" numbers, I uncovered some remarkable facts and figures. During that season, each week the number one-ranked team lost five times, while the number two-ranked team lost seven times. That means that for the fourteen-week season, the number one-ranked team was upset 35.7% of the time and the number two-ranked team was upset 50% of the time.

I then took a look at the top ten rankings and found that the top ten ranked teams collectively lost 24% of the time. On September 30, 2007, 50% of the top ten teams lost. That was followed up on October 7, October 21, and November 25 with 40% of the top ten teams losing.

Even the 2007-08 bowl games held true to upset form. From December 20, 2007, to January 7, 2008, thirty-two bowl games were played. Winning a bowl game is huge. The resultant media attention enhances recruiting, and the monetary payouts are sizeable. That year's payout totaled a whopping $125,900,000. Up to two months of extra preparation by all involved went into each of these games. The dream of the upset was realized by eight of the thirty-two teams. That's a 25% upset rate. It seemed fitting that the bowl games reflected the regular season — the "Season of the Upset." In each case, however, it took someone, or a group of "someones" to believe in the dream. They worked their dream to the point that when hard work and preparation met opportunity, the collision created the upset.

The NFL is not immune to the upset, either. As a matter of fact, it is rife with hundreds of storied upset wins. Just to illustrate the point, let me share with you some interesting statistics from the 1990 to the 2005 NFL seasons. "NFL Angles" did some research on opening day upsets in the NFL. They used as their criteria the betting line to determine which were the favored teams and which were the underdogs. Expansion teams were excluded in this profile. Over the entire sixteen-year span of the study, on average, there were 2.25 upsets per opening day in the NFL. Based on past performance, the math tells us that with sixteen opening games played between the thirty-two NFL teams, approximately 14%, or one out of every seven games, will result in an upset. Granted, not all of these NFL upsets are major stories, but it does prove the maxim, "The best team does not always win." You just need to be the best team that day!

The 2008 Super Bowl (Super Bowl XLII) game between the New York Giants and the New England Patriots was a fitting climax to the 2007-08 "Season of the Upset." In the game that many pundits call one of the best Super Bowl games ever, the New York Giants beat the New England Patriots 17-14. The Patriots, often described as possibly the best NFL team of all time, were undefeated. The Giants were a clear twelve-point underdog led by still unproven quarterback Eli Manning. Comparisons of the two teams were always unfavorable to the Giants, but when the time came to play it out on the field of battle, the results were surprising. The Giants managed an eighty-three yard two-minute drill that resulted in a winning touchdown pass. The most spectacular play in that last series will probably be remembered as one of the most incredible plays in Super Bowl history. Eli Manning's scramble from a host of Patriot defenders and the unbelievable thirty-yard catch by David Tyree kept the winning drive alive and energized the crowd.

Guard Rich Seubert should also be mentioned in the telling of this story. Seubert was initially beaten at the snap, but his no-quit hustle enabled him to regroup and get a key block to free Manning from the grip of several defenders. This was an upset that was not the result of the "superior" team being unprepared or playing poorly. This was a hard-fought slugfest between two teams that refused to quit. Because it was so hotly contested, the Giants' win is even more unbelievable. Unbelievable, that is, to the millions of us who thought the Patriots would win, but not unbelievable to the Giants' coaching staff and players. They had a vision that they would win. They believed in their coaches and each other. They took the vision and the belief and made it happen! They truly made the "art of the upset" come to life.

GREAT UPSETS IN MILITARY HISTORY

I taught history for thirty-one years. During that time I came across some outstanding examples of historical military upsets that I feel are more than worthy of mention. Not all of the illustrations that you share with your team need to be football stories. I have found that the military examples have tremendous impact because they help to reinforce the idea that upsets can and do happen! They also show real-life application to the principles that you are teaching. Let me give you a few good examples.

The challenge faced by the "300 Spartans" at Thermopylae, who held off a Persian army estimated to be sixty times their size, provides one of the greatest examples of an "upset" that one can find. Even though it was a tactical victory for the Persians, it was a tremendous moral victory for the Greeks. This battle in 480 BC has become synonymous with the overcoming of great odds. The three hundred Spartans, bolstered by approximately seven hundred now-forgotten Thespians, were determined to hold the pass against the Persians at all costs. Their mission was to delay the Persians and allow for the safe retreat of the main Greek army. They lost their lives but accomplished their task.

If you analyze their "victory" it resembles a football game in some respects. The Spartans were the superior trained and conditioned "team." They obtained good field position (the pass) and devised a great game plan – the use of the phalanx. They fought with high morale and a "never quit" attitude. The reality of the situation was that they could not win, but they chose to go with their own internal reality rather than the external one. They were so positive in their quest that they ignored every negative factor and concentrated only on the goal. Herodotus in his book *Histories* wrote that when Dienekes, a Spartan soldier, was informed that Persian arrows were so numerous that they blotted out the sun, he remarked, "So much the better, we shall fight in the shade." Now that's positive thinking! It was reported that when their spears broke, the Spartans fought hand-to-hand with their short swords. When they too broke, they fought with bare hands, teeth, and nails. They fought until the last man went down.

That's just the way we wanted our team to "fight" in the game. We wanted them to give their all and never quit. We wanted them to fight full force until the final gun sounded at the end of the game, with no energy left untapped—totally spent in effort. Regardless of the score, for us that would be a victory, just as it was for the "300 Spartans" almost 2,500 years ago.

From the Civil War, a great example to share with your team is Stonewall Jackson's incredible Shenandoah Valley campaign of 1862. Jackson pressed his army to travel on foot 646 miles in 48 days of marching and won five significant victories against three separate Union armies. He did all of this with a force of about 17,000 against a combined Union force of 60,000 men. Now that's moving it! If Jackson's men had been a football team, we would have assigned it the acronym: "HAM." For us, "HAM" meant "Hostile, Agile, and Mobile."

The battle for Guadalcanal during World War II was always special to me because a personal friend, Marine Sergeant Jack Frayne, who survived this nightmare (malaria, multiple bullet and fragment injuries), could personally relate this upset to our students and athletes. Jack, a true and highly decorated WWII hero, was a living link to the August 7, 1942, to February 7, 1943, operation. Through his teaching, he made the event truly come to life. Eleven thousand marines landed on the South Solomon island of Guadalcanal. During the landing, the Allied forces lost one destroyer and nineteen aircraft. However, on the second night our ships were heavily attacked, resulting in the sinking of four cruisers, with damage to one cruiser and two destroyers. A decision was made to remove our fleet from the area by the third night. This left much of the heavy equipment, provisions, and remaining troops still aboard the transports. With only a fourteen-day supply of food, the Marines were eventually reduced to eating only small cups of rice and coconuts. Dysentery and tropical disease soon took their toll. Japanese reinforcements had our troops fighting for their lives. Displaying individual and collective acts of heroism, our troops never quit and held their ground against increasing odds. Their valiant efforts resulted in the first significant strategic victory by Allied forces over Japanese forces in the Pacific theatre. We were finally able to move off the defensive and begin the offensive campaign that would lead to the ultimate defeat of Japan and the end of World War II. For this reason the Guadalcanal campaign is often referred to as a great historical "upset" and the "turning point" in the war.

Another significant "upset" was General Douglas MacArthur's

miraculous landing invasion at Inchon, September 15, 1950, during the Korean War. This example actually fits into two categories. The Inchon invasion certainly can be classified as an upset, but also as a "trick play," as well. MacArthur, through the dissemination of counter-intelligence, feigned one way and then did the totally unexpected by taking a route that no one could have ever predicted. If you had to choose an invasion landing spot, Inchon, South Korea, would be last on the list. It features high sea walls to be scaled, currents up to eight knots, and tide changes of thirty feet (the second highest tide change in the world). But in just four days, MacArthur succeeded in landing 6,629 vehicles, 53,882 troops, and 25,512 pounds of supplies. Now that's another example of what Civil War general William Tecumseh Sherman called getting there the "fastest with the mostest." The Battle of Inchon ended a string of victories by the invading North Korean army and began a counter-attack by United Nations forces that led to the recapture of Seoul.

Let me give you one final "upset" example from military history as described in James D. Hornfischer's book *The Last Stand of the Tin Can Sailors*. During the naval conflict with Japan in World War II, near the Philippine Island of Samar, a small task force of U.S. aircraft carriers found themselves in the sights of a Japanese armada. The thirteen-ship task force (Taffy 3) consisted of six light carriers and seven destroyers. The Japanese fleet pursuing them consisted of a fighting force of four mammoth battleships, six heavy cruisers, two light cruisers, and eleven destroyers. The Japanese battle ship *Yamato* (the most powerful battleship in the world at that time) was capable of firing 18.1-inch shells that were six and one-half feet long and weighed 3219 pounds. Their range was an astonishing 26 miles. The best the U.S. destroyers protecting the aircraft carriers could do was a range of 6 miles maximum, with much smaller ordinance. For any real impact, they had to be almost at point-blank range.

What ensued in the course of two and one-half hours on October 25, 1944, can best be described by historian Samuel Eliot Morison: "In no engagement in its entire history has the United States Navy shown more gallantry, guts, and gumption than in those two morning hours . . . off Samar."

It was a modern version of the David and Goliath story. The odds were impossible to calculate. There was no way that this small task force could prevent the Japanese strike force from blowing right through them and heading for the vulnerable MacArthur-led Philippine Liberation Forces. Although the situation was apparently hopeless, instead of running, the U.S. destroyers turned and headed straight for the Japanese ships. This surprise move so startled the Japanese fleet that the U.S. destroyers were able to get in close and outmaneuver the larger and heavier enemy ships. Their valiant efforts thwarted the attack and saved the U.S. carriers and the Liberation Forces.

Many sacrificed their lives to accomplish this upset. I don't know how to describe the heroic and gallant performance of these men, but I do know that they conquered their fears and rose far and above the call of duty that day. They pulled off the biggest upset in U.S. Naval warfare history. That battle and the three days of ensuing melees, author, James D. Hornfischer believes, were " . . . by multiple measures the most sprawling, spectacular, and horrible naval battle in history° It was the greatest naval battle ever fought for the distances it spanned, for the tonnage of ships sunk, for the duration of the duels between surface ships, and for the terrible losses of human life." Herman Wouk wrote in *War and Remembrance*, "The vision of

Sprague's three destroyers . . . charging out of the smoke and rain straight toward the main batteries of Kurita's battleships and cruisers, can endure as a picture of the way Americans fight when they don't have superiority. Our school children should know about that incident, and our enemies should ponder it."

Your team should know about it, too. Stories about real people in real-life situations doing the unthinkable serve a purpose. These examples provide inspiration and validity to your assertion to your team that they too can pull off the upset. Our upsets pale in comparison to these stories, but our "big game" is our Battle of Samar. From these true epic stories we can learn about "the way Americans fight when they don't have superiority."

Can you make these stories come to life for your players? That's the important thing. Use the stories to illustrate the human drama within the event. These were real people faced with unbelievable odds. They found the will and the way to fight and win. It can be done. This is by no means a complete list of "upset" and inspirational stories from history, but they are a good sampling of some of my favorite ones.

POLITICAL UPSETS
"Up Close and Personal"

The basic philosophy of how to pull off the great football upset is applicable to any profession or walk of life. I found this to be especially true in my other career as a State Representative for the state of Delaware.

When I first decided to run for a seat in the state Legislature, my party had never won in my residential and electoral district. To make matters worse, at that time the seat was held by a popular incumbent. The party registration percentages were abysmal and daunting. My party was outnumbered by a 5-to-1 ratio. It would have been easy to concede defeat even before the race had begun! But just as in my football career, I was blessed with great people to help me in the campaign. I had the dynamic duo of Jackie and Doug Brown as my political mentors. Jackie was the Colonial Region chairperson, and Doug was my campaign manager. I added my coaching buddy Dave Taylor as my treasurer, and we were set to go.

Thanks to great preparation by Jackie and Doug and many a mile walked on the campaign trail, we slowly eroded the numerical advantage of my opponent. My family also got into the act. My wife and family helped by going door-to-door, and my father handled the construction and placement of the campaign signs. Sandy Dwyer, who was my football team's Booster president and later, the party's District chairperson, worked along with many other friends and teaching colleagues manning the phone lines and staffing our campaign headquarters. I do believe that we left no stone unturned. Several of my political friends also helped canvass door-to-door. This is not a complete list of those who helped. The number of helpers is truly too large to name each and every one, but their contributions were immensely beneficial.

The margin of victory was slim, but it was definitely an upset victory. Perseverance, hard work, great staff, and a belief that we would win propelled that initial campaign. We built a great team. We even called our political committee "Team to Elect Reynolds." We ran it just the way a successful football program should be run, and it worked.

But I have also been on the losing side of football games and political campaigns. When analyzed, the losses can be attributed to a breakdown in the fundamentals to the "art of the upset." I lost some close games and elections because I did *not* leave every stone unturned. I did *not* follow every principle that I have espoused in this book. I have to admit, though, that some losses occurred because the other team or opponent was just better that day. You have to give credit when others work hard and pull off the upset against you, but that still illustrates my point. Follow the principles outlined in *Art of the Upset* and you will upset many more opponents than will upset you. I won nine elections in my eighteen-year career as a Representative, and served as chairman of the House Education Committee. We won seven state football championships and finished second four times during that time. "The proof is in the pudding"!

One other political story is even more remarkable. Terry Spence was a Delaware neighbor and still is a good friend. He also has been a Representative in the Delaware Legislature. His story offers an outstanding example of how great things can happen when you believe in yourself and work to make them happen. Terry did not go to college directly from high school; while working for the DuPont Company, he went back to school and got his college degree. That was not easy with four children and a full-time job! Terry will be the first to tell you that his wife Nancy deserves a lot of the credit for this accomplishment. He also ran for political office. Facing overwhelming registration odds, he lost in his first attempt, but it did not deter him. He learned from the loss and vowed to run an even better campaign the next time. He did, and he won. He not only did that, but he moved up the leadership chain of command in the House of Representatives. In 1986 he was elected by his peers to the highest position in the House–he became the Speaker of the House. According to the 2008 *Handbook of State Legislative Leaders*, he holds the record for being the longest continuously sitting Speaker of the House in the history of the nation. That's an amazing accomplishment! Terry has a natural charisma, but it was hard work that put him where he is today. He truly cares about helping others and has logged many a mile by foot and by car to personally serve his constituents. When you look at the odds that were initially against him, it makes his accomplishment an "upset" of the highest magnitude.

I like sharing these non-sport stories of upsets for many reasons. They provided inspiration to our players. They were used as illustrations for our program philosophy and the "art of the upset." But it was also our goal that when we taught our philosophy of the "upset," it would translate into a life-lesson (one that could be applied to any situation in life). We wanted our players to be able to apply what they learned from our program to their careers, relationships, hardships, failures, and successes. I used these personal and local examples because I felt it was important for our players to see that our philosophy has worked with people that they know.

I shared with our team my own political story and Terry Spence's for another reason as well. We both played football and are alumni of William Penn High School. We were one of them.

EPILOGUE

The principles applied in *Art of the Upset* are not limited to use in football alone. They translate to any sport and to almost any walk of life. As an educator, I tried to follow these principles with all of my students. Motivation and inspiration are essential ingredients in helping students achieve, whether on the playing field or in the classroom. From the high achiever to the student with learning disabilities, the fundamentals remain the same. It takes your best effort to guide young students in their quest for academic success. It is even more important to apply these fundamentals to those students who are totally unmotivated or hostile to the school environment. You will never win them all, but you will be surprised at the successes that do result. Even if you reach only one reluctant learner, isn't that worthwhile? There is an old proverb that comes to mind: "It is better to light one small candle than to forever curse the darkness."

I hope you have found ideas you can use in *Art of the Upset*. I have enjoyed sharing with you a lifetime of observations, interactions, stories, and life-lessons that have come together to produce this book. My hope is that you will apply the philosophy that is inherent in this book to your own team and to your own life. The "never quit" theme is at the heart of success and is the key to the upset. Armed with this knowledge, you too can "Dare to Dream."

AUTHOR'S NOTE REGARDING SOURCES IN *ART OF THE UPSET*

Over the years, I collected many of the brief quotations and inspirational stories shared in *Art of the Upset* as I encountered them listening to speakers at conferences and in casual reading of inspirational articles. In many cases, the identity of the original author or speaker has disappeared as stories were circulated throughout the coaching community. Often, when a source was identified, it was the ubiquitous "Anonymous" who takes credit for much of the wisdom in the world. I have identified these sources to the best of my knowledge within the text.

Other print and online sources are listed at the end of the book. The reader usually will find an author or speaker mentioned in the text, and should be able to match the name given with an entry on the Works Cited list.

There are numerous sources for inspirational quotations available on the World Wide Web, and any single quotation is likely to show up on several sites, sometimes with slight variations. The online sources listed on the Works Cited page were active at the time of publication.

WORKS CITED

Bennet, William [quoted in] Fisher, R. McKenzie. *Lessons from the Gridiron*. New Leaf, 1995.

Bielat, Larry. *Winning Words*. Sports Art, 1984.

Bristol, Claude. *The Magic of Believing*. Simon, 1985.

Brown, Steve. *A Scandalous Freedom*. Howard, 2004.

Carnegie, Dale. *How to Win Friends and Influence People*. Simon, 1981.

Cohen, William A. "The Eight Keys to Leadership Greatness." *JAS Coaching and Training Newsletter*. Ed. Janine Schindler. Jan. 2008 http://www.jascoaching.com/newsletter0108.html.

Collins, Jim. *Good to Great*. Harper Business, 2001.

Conwell, Russell, William George Jordan, and James Allen. *Motivational Classics*. Ed. Charles Jones. Executive, 1983. Includes three books: *Acres of Diamonds* (Conwell), *The Kingship of Self Control* (Jordan), and *As a Man Thinketh* (Allen).

Courage to Conquer. Ed. Leroy King. Revell, 1966.

Covey, Stephen. *The Seven Habits of Highly Effective People*. Simon, 1989.

Herrick, Thaddeus. "Leadership as Layup? Everything You Need to Know about Management You Can Learn on the Court." *Wall Street Journal* 14 Mar. 2005: R10.

Hornfischer, James D. *The Last Stand of the Tin Can Sailors*. Bantam, 2005.

Krzyzewski, Mike. *Beyond Basketball*. Warner, 2006.

—. *Leading with the Heart*. Warner, 2000.

Marston, Ralph S., Jr. *The Daily Motivator to Go*. Image Express, 1997.

Maxwell, John C. *The Twenty-one Indispensable Qualities of a Leader*. Nelson, 1999.

McCasland, David C. "True Victory." *Our Daily Bread*. Ed. Tim Gustafson. RBC Global Ministries. 13 Nov. 2006 http://www.rbc.org /devotionals/our-daily-bread/2006/11/13/devotion.aspx.

Neill, James. "Quotes by and about Kurt Hahn." *Wilderdom*. 3 Jan. 2009 http://wilderdom.com/Hahn.htm.

Peale, Norman Vincent. *The Power of Positive Thinking*. Simon, 2003.

Roosevelt, Theodore. *History as Literature*. Scribner, 1913. 4 Jan. 2009 http://www.bartleby.com/56/.

Schwartz, David J. *The Magic of Thinking Big*. Simon, 1987.

Shepard, Greg. *Be an Eleven: Guidebook for Success*. Bigger Faster Stronger, 2002.

Siris, Peter. *Guerrilla Investing: Winning Strategies for Beating the Wall Street Professionals*. Longstreet, 2000.

Smedes, Lewis. *Forgive and Forget: Healing the Hurts We Don't Deserve*. Harper, 1996.

Smith, Jeffrey D. *Focus on Your Dream*. Possibility, 2003.

Success. Ed. Jena Pincott. Random, 2005.

Torre, Joe. *Joe Torre's Ground Rules for Winners*. Hyperion, 1999.

Waitzkin, Josh. *The Art of Learning*. Free, 2007.

Willingham, Tyrone [quoted in] Riach, Steve. *Amazing but True Sports Stories*. Hallmark, 2004.

Wooden, John. *They Call Me Coach*. McGraw, 2003.

Wouk, Herman. *War and Remembrance*. Little, 2002.

Ziglar, Zig. *Breaking Through to the Next Level*. Honor, 1998.

—. *Great Quotes from Zig Ziglar*. Career, 1997.

The following Web sites are also sources of quotations cited throughout *Art of the Upset*:

The Quotations Page: http://quotationspage.com/

Quoteland.com: http://www.quoteland.com/

ThinkExist.com: http://thinkexist.com/